Castles of Kent

Bruce W. Johnson

Castles of Kent

Copyright December 2022

All rights reserved.

No part of this work may be reproduced, stored in a retrieval system or transmitted in any form or by any means without the prior permission, in writing, of the copyright holder.

Bruce W. Johnson

Dedication

This book is dedicated to my wife, who has shared with me the enjoyment of so many beautiful places.

Castles of Kent

Cover Image: Saint Leonard's Tower, West Malling.

Bruce W. Johnson

Contents

List of Maps 6
Exploring Castles 7
The Castles of Kent 8
Castle by Castle 13
Minor Castle Sites 194
Planning your visits 195
Places to stay 211
Weddings and Venues 213
Cycle Repairs 214
List of Illustrations 215
Acknowledgements 218

List of Maps

Castles of Kent	Page	10
Map of the Saxon Shore Forts in Kent	Page	136
Touring North Kent	Page	199
Touring East Kent	Page	201
Touring West Kent	Page	203
The Very Best Castles in Kent	Page	205
Touring Kent Castle Gardens	Page	207

Bruce W. Johnson

Exploring Castles

There have been many books on castles, but this one is intended to be rather different. In recent years a new word has entered the English language, as increasing numbers of people have begun to discover the joys of taking a "Staycation" rather than a foreign holiday.

The British Isles enjoy a rich cultural heritage, including many magnificent castles, palaces and stately homes. The most famous of these host thousands of visitors every year, and yet, even in this age of information overload, many of the best attractions are largely undiscovered, tucked away just a few miles off the main road. There is a real danger that we drive or cycle a considerable distance to visit one attraction, but miss out on three or four others in the local area. My aim, therefore, is to offer the reader more options and more information, so as to help visitors get more out of their holidays.

I have attempted to include all of the information that visitors might find useful, not only the history and design of the castle itself, but also post codes and road numbers for navigation, routes for tours and details of other things to see and do in the local area.

There are even some places where it is possible to spend a few romantic nights actually living as a guest in a castle or to book one as a glittering wedding venue.

My dearest wish, in publishing this book, is that when you explore these wonderful castles you will get the greatest possible enjoyment from your visit.

Bruce W. Johnson 2022

The Castles of Kent

Allington Castle	ME16 0NB	Maidstone
Bayford Castle	ME10 3JQ	Sittingbourne
Binbury Castle	ME14 3HU	Sittingbourne
Brenchley Manor	TN12 7NS	Tonbridge
Brenchley Castle	TN12 7BW	Tonbridge
Bromley Castle	BR2 0EN	Bromley
Bromley Palace	BR1 3UH	Bromley
Canterbury Castle	CT1 2PR	Canterbury
Castle Rough	ME10 2TU	Sittingbourne
Castle Toll	TN18 5PY	Newenden
Chiddingstone	TN8 7AH	Edenbridge
Chilham	CT4 8DB	Canterbury
Colebridge Farm	TN27 9BP	Egerton
Cooling Gatehouse	ME3 8DT	Hoo peninsula
Deal Castle	CT14 7BA	Deal
Dover Castle	CT16 1HU	Dover
Dymchurch Redoubt	DA4 0AA	Hythe
Eastwell Manor	TN25 4HR	Ashford
Eynesford Castle	DA4 0AA	Swanley
Fairseat Castle	ME19 5EG	West Malling
Folkestone Castle	CT19 5LP	Folkestone
Fort Amherst	ME4 4UB	Gillingham
Garlinge Castle	CT9 5LL	Margate
Gundulph's Tower	ME1 1SX	Rochester
Hadlow Castle	TN11 0ED	Tonbridge
Hever Castle	TN8 7NG	Sevenoaks
Ightham Mote	TN15 0NT	Sevenoaks
Kingsgate	CT10 3PH	Broadstairs
Knole	TN15 0HT	Sevenoaks
Knox Bridge Castle	TN17 2BT,	Knox Bridge
Leeds Castle	ME17 1PL	Maidstone
Leybourne Castle	ME19 5HD	Maidstone
Lullingstone Castle	DA4 0AJ	Sevenoaks
Lympne Castle	CT21 4LQ	Folkestone
Newnham Castle	ME9 0JX	Sittingbourne

Mereworth Castle	ME18 5JB	Maidstone
Old Soar	TN15 0QX	Sevenoaks
Old Walmer Court	CT14 7RP	Walmer
Otford Palace	TN14 5PG	Sevenoaks
Penshurst Place	TN11 8DG	Tonbridge
Queenborough	ME11 5DD	Sheppey
Reculver	CT6 6SS	Canterbury
Richborough	CT13 9JH	Sandwich,
Rochester	ME1 1QQ	Rochester
St Leonards Tower	ME19 6PD	West Malling
Saltwood Castle	CT21 4QU	Hythe
Sandgate Castle	CT20 3RR	Sandgate
Sandown Castle	CT14 6NY	Sandown
Sandwich	CT13 9EA	Sandwich
Scotney Castle	TN3 8JN	Tonbridge Wells
Severndroog	SE18 3RT	London
Shoreham Castle	TN14 7UD	Lullingstone
Shurland Hall	ME12 4BN	Isle of Sheppey
Sissinghurst Castle	TN17 2AB	Ashford
Starkey Castle	ME1 3TR	Medway
Stockbury Castle	ME9 7RD	Sittingbourne,
Stone Castle	DA9 9XL	Greenhithe
Stutfall Castle	CT21 4LQ	Hythe
Sutton Valence	ME17 3BS	Sutton Valence
Thurnham Castle	ME14 3LE	Maidstone
Tonbridge Castle	TN9 1BG	Tonbridge
Tonge Castle	ME9 9AP	Sittingbourne
Upnor Castle	ME2 4XG	Medway
Vanbrugh	SE10 8XQ	Greenwich
Walmer Castle	CT14 7LJ	Walmer
Westenhanger Castle	CT21 4HX	Hythe
Whitstable	CT5 2BW	Whitstable

Castles of Kent

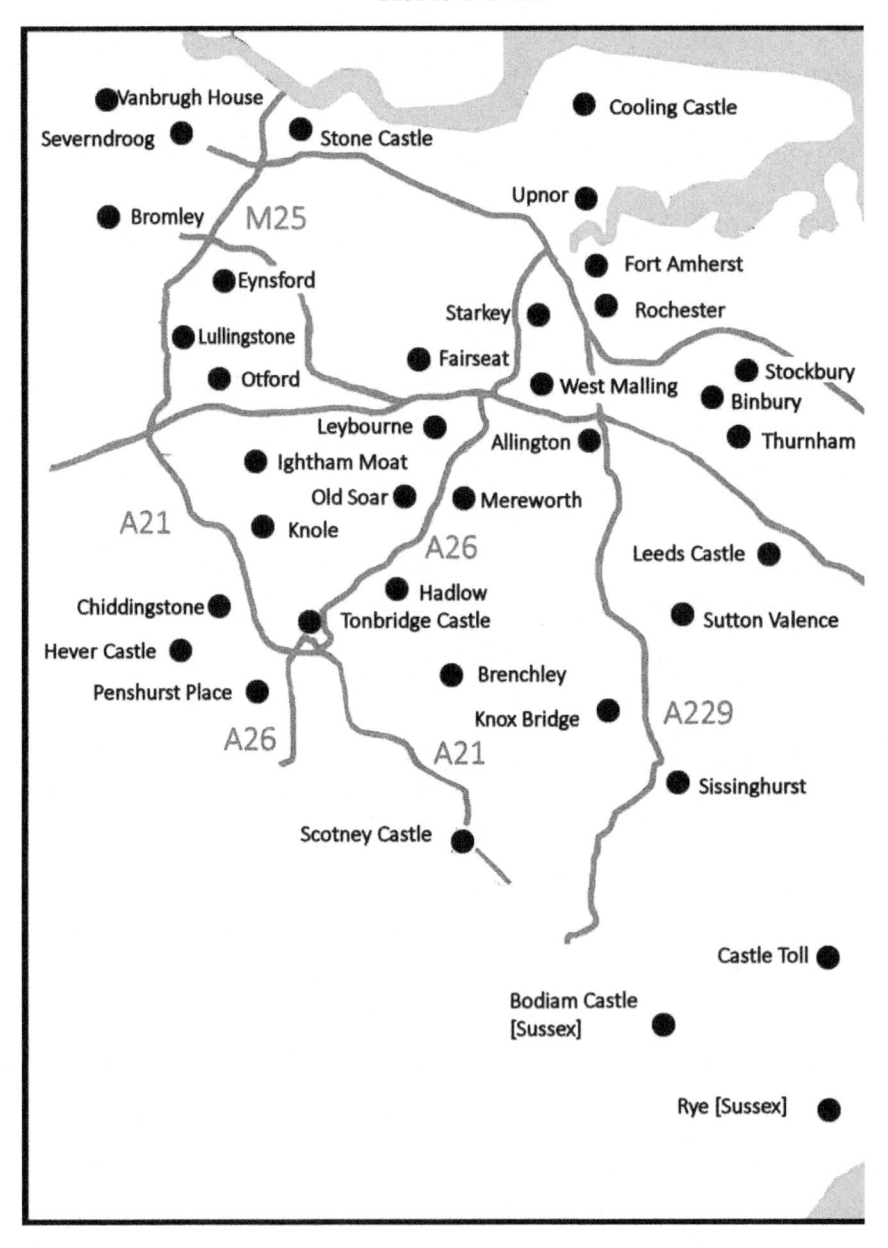

The Castles of Kent

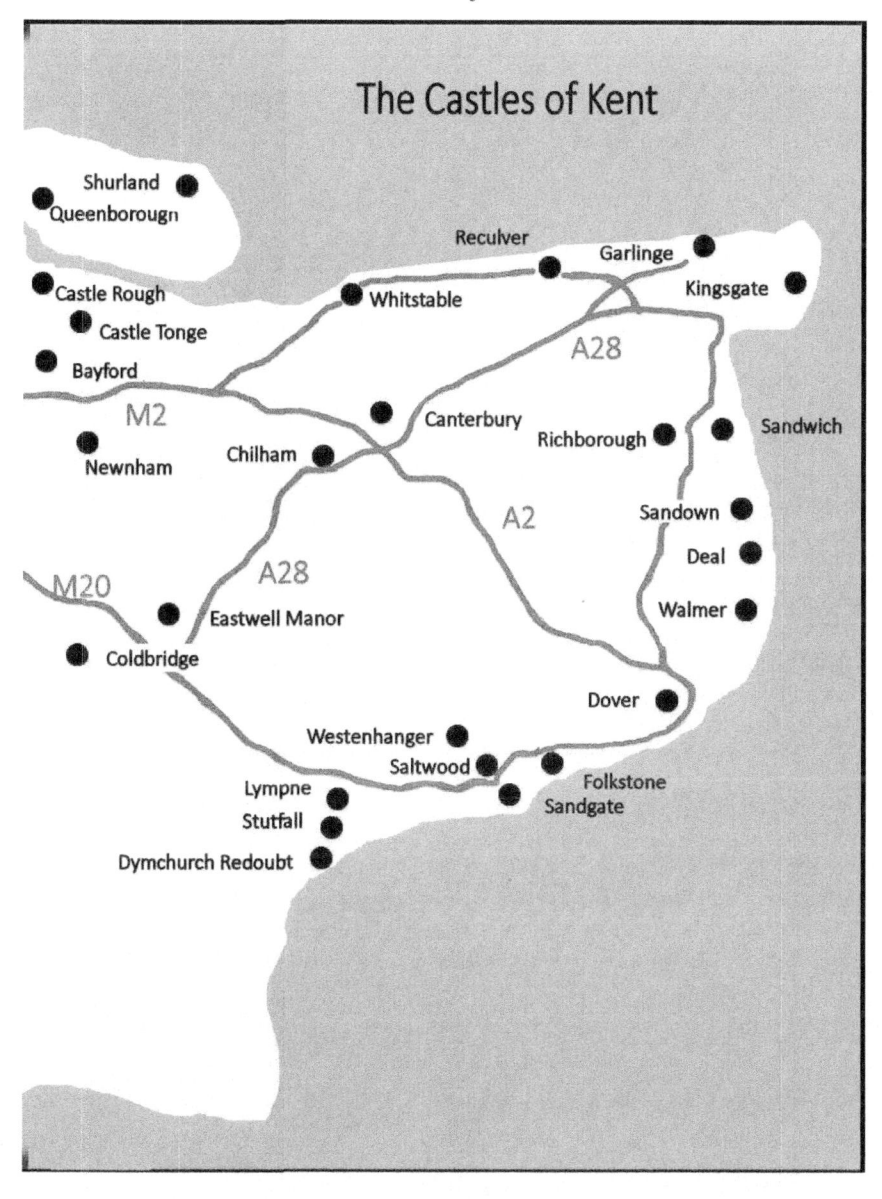

- Shurland
- Queenborough
- Castle Rough
- Castle Tonge
- Bayford
- Newnham
- Reculver
- Whitstable
- Garlinge
- Kingsgate
- Canterbury
- Chilham
- Richborough
- Sandwich
- Sandown
- Deal
- Walmer
- Eastwell Manor
- Coldbridge
- Dover
- Westenhanger
- Saltwood
- Lympne
- Folkstone
- Sandgate
- Stutfall
- Dymchurch Redoubt

The Weavers Cottages, Canterbury

In addition to its wonderful castles, Kent has much to offer tourists.

Tudor Red-Brick buildings in Rochester High Street

Bruce W. Johnson

Castle by Castle

The following pages form a gazetteer of those castles which tourists may wish to visit. Please do remember that some of the sites have little left in the way of remains. In order to avaoid disappointment, always read the description of the site before starting a journey.

Allington Castle

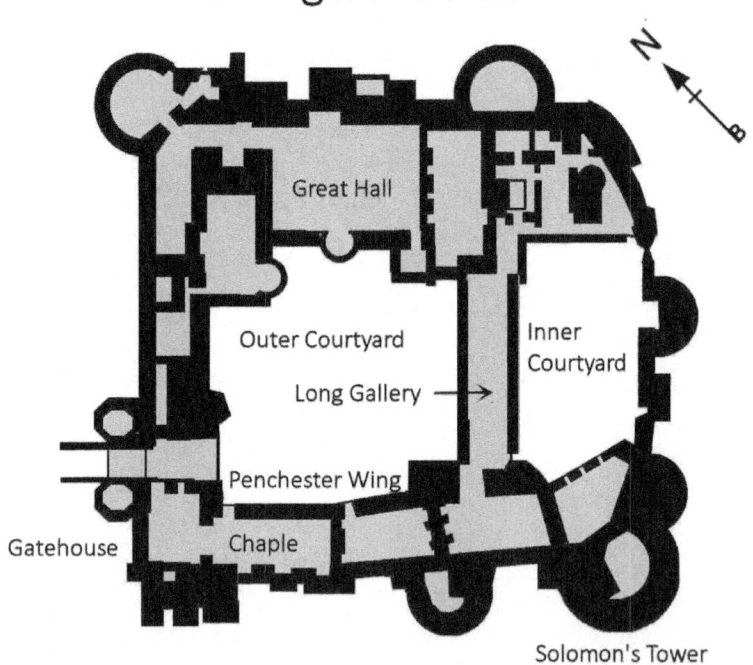

- Great Hall
- Outer Courtyard
- Inner Courtyard
- Long Gallery
- Penchester Wing
- Gatehouse
- Chaple
- Solomon's Tower

10 Metres

Bruce W. Johnson

Allington Castle

A major structure, near Maidstone. Privately owned
Postcode for Satnav: ME16 0NB
Nearest major road   M20
Website: https://allington-castle.com/
Parking Arrangements by arrangement

Also nearby
St. Leonard's Tower, West Malling
Aylesford Priory.
Bluebell Hill [Local beauty spot]

Allington castle is not open to the public. I would not advise you to make a trip to visit it as there is little to see from the road, merely a back gate. In years gone by a few intrepid photographers have managed to take photographs from the towpath along the river bank, but there are few opportunities now, as the view is largely obscured by dense hedges.

Description and Defences
Allington is shaped like a large capital 'D' with six round towers projecting from the walls. On the outside it was surrounded by a moat. The original courtyard has been bisected by the Tudor Long Gallery

There is an excellent gatehouse which would once have had both a portcullis and a drawbridge. Solomon's tower in the south-west corner is especially strong and could be used as a keep. In medieval times it was where the troops or guards lived.

History
Allington Castle was originally a manor house and was upgraded to a moated motte and bailey castle by Sir William De Warenne, 2nd Earl of Surrey, during the early 12th century. This was a troubled period in English History which featured a long-running civil war between King Stephen and the Empress Matilda. As the castle did not have royal approval, King Henry II later ordered it to be demolished and it became, once more, a manor house.

The present castle was then built between 1279 and 1299 by Sir Stephen De Pencester, the Lord Warden of the Cinque Ports, who had been granted a licence to crenellate, by King Edward I, in 1282. Unusually, for a medieval castle, some of the building work was carried out in brick, rather than stone.

As the name implies, Pencester also owned Penshurst Place, another of Kent's most famous stately homes.

Allington later passed, by marriage, to the Cobham family and was expanded during the 13th century. In 1492 the castle came into the hands of Sir Henry Wyatt. King Henry VII was secure on the throne and the Wars of the Roses had been over for seven years. From this time onwards the castle was used more as a stately home than as a military stronghold. Wyatt is believed to have built the "long gallery" which cut the courtyard into two separate sections. These long galleries were a particular favourite in Tudor times. When the weather outside was unfavourable, aristocratic families would exercise themselves and entertain their guests by walking up and down their gallery, as an alternative to walking round the gardens.

The galleries would often be decorated with portraits of family members, intended to impress their neighbours by showing that they had a noble pedigree, and were rich enough to have their portraits painted!

King Henry VII and his son Henry VIII are both known to have visited Allington Castle, as well as Cardinal Wolsey, Anne Boleyn, and Catherine Parr. There is actually a room in the north-east tower which served as a guest room and has been known as the "Royal Room" ever since.

Allington Castle in 1909

Henry VIII was always extremely anxious regarding his own personal safety, fearing assassination plots. It is said that whenever he stayed at Allington he had workers build a dry-stone wall at the bottom of the stairway to keep out anyone who might do him harm, and then each morning the workers would have to take the wall down again. This may seem difficult to believe but we know that there were other castles where he had the locks replaced with his own locks for the duration of his stay, so this somewhat paranoid behaviour is quite possibly true.

In 1537 Sir Thomas Wyatt inherited the castle but around the same time it was revealed that he had been a lover of Anne Boleyn before she married the king and he was imprisoned in the tower of London, This could easily have cost him both his life and his property. In fact he was soon released from the tower and banished to his estate at Allington, which was not confiscated. Eventually seems that the king forgave him completely and even allowed him some of the local lands which arose from the dissolution of the monasteries, including one at Aylesford.

Wyatt seems to have been very lucky, in an age when people had their heads chopped off for a great deal less. The most likely explanation is that the King had known all along about the affair, but felt obliged to make a bit of a show about it.

Allington Castle in 2022

Sir Thomas Wyatt the younger inherited the castle in 1541. Being a staunch protestant he was involved in a protestant plot and rebellion against the Catholic Queen Mary. In fact the plotters held their first meeting at the castle. When the rebellion failed Thomas Wyatt was executed and the estate, including the castle, was confiscated and it became crown property in 1554. With their fortunes ruined, the rest of the Wyatt family left England for the new colonies in the Americas.

Queen Elizabeth I granted the castle to Sir John Astley in 1570 but he seems to have chosen to spend little time there. Over the next hundred years the castle had little money spent on it and fell into disrepair. Things then went from bad to worse when the main building was gutted by fire.

In the 17th century the Best family purchased the castle and made a number of alterations. Being Roman Catholics they had a private chapel and even a "priest hole" in the gatehouse, where a visiting priest could hide during the religious turbulence of the civil war period.

The castle was purchased by Sir Robert Marsham in 1720 and its dilapidated appearance was captured by Turner in several pieces of artwork produced in 1798.

In the 19th Century the building suffered another fire and some of its stones were robbed as building materials.

At the beginning of the 20th Century the castle purchased by Lord Conway for £4800, and together with his American wife, Katrina, he set about having the building tastefully restored it in a style compatible with its age. In this, no doubt, they benefitted from the fact that their daughter Agnes was an archaeologist.

The full restoration took around 30 years and was completed by 1932, it included the reconstruction of the long gallery which had been for the most part destroyed.

Lord Conway himself produced a comprehensive written study of the buildings which can still be read on the website of the Kent Archaeological Society: www.kentarchaeology.org.uk (then search for Allington 19090

Agnes Conway owned the castle until her death in 1950, at which point it was sold off for £15,000 to a group of Roman Catholic Nuns, the Order of Carmelites, connected to Aylesford Priory which lies nearby. Thus Allington became a religious community, a situation which continued until 1999. It became a Grade I listed building in 1951.

In recent years the castle has been the home of Sir Robert Worcester, the founder of the MORI polling company.

The restoration work which took place in the early twentieth century was carried out to an exceptionally high standard. As a result the entire castle is both tasteful and authentic.

At the time of writing [2022] the castle is available to hire for filming, conferences and high quality wedding receptions. See the castle's official website for details. The great hall, with its timbered ceiling, is in excellent condition and as a result the castle is an exceptional venue for functions.

Allington Castle: The Medieval Great Hall

Bayford Castle

A minor structure, near Sittingbourne.
Postcode for Satnav: ME14 3HU
Nearest major road   A2 / M2

Some locals believe that this site may have originally been a Roman Army marching camp. Others say that King Alfred the Great may have built a fortified camp on this site when on campaign against the Danish invaders. There is little to see now except some earthworks, ridges and dips in the earth, now overgrown with trees, in the middle of an industrial estate. I would not particularly recommend this site as a place to visit unless you just happen to be passing, or have a particular interest the archaeology of the period.

History
By Norman times there was a wooden motte and bailey castle at Bayford and a nearby manor house was believed to have been owned by Earl Godwin, father of King Harold Godwinson.

Bayford Castle and Goodmanston (Goodneston, Godewynston) were separate manors but from c.1368, it appears that both were held by Sir Robert de Nottingham, who resided at Bayford who used the Latin phrase "apud castellum suum de Bayford, apud Goodneston" on his documents. From this it may be conjectured that his main house was at Bayford manor whilst the Goodmanston Manor House gradually became less important.

Eventually the Bayford site became the property of the Cheyney family and was later owned by Sir William Garrard, the Mayor of London, though by this time it was only a farmhouse.

Description and Defences
The site is a square enclosure with a moat up to 30ft wide, which can still sometimes fill up with tidal seawater. There were remains of buildings but they seem to have disappeared around the year 1800.

Bruce W. Johnson

Binbury Castle

A minor structure, near Sittingbourne.
Postcode for Satnav: ME14 3HU
Nearest major road   A2 / M2

Variously known as Bonbury Castle, Bengebury and also Stockings Wood Castle. There is very little left of the castle, only part of one tower which has become part of the farmhouse. I would not particularly recommend this site as a place to visit unless you just happen to be passing, or have a particular interest the archaeology of the period.

History

This structure started out as a Saxon hunting lodge and was later rebuilt as an early motte and bailey castle, albeit on a very small scale.

A rather strange event was reported near to the castle in the year 1340;

"And, afterwards, viz. in the month of January, in the thirteenth year of the reign of King Edward III., the same Sir Roger contracted a third marriage, viz. with Margaret, relict of Sir Nicholas de Halglton, Knight, lord of Wokyndon in the county of Essex, who had two daughters, Beatrice, now the wife of Sir Ralph Seynt-leger, Knight, and Margaret, who was married to Sir Roger de Northwode, son of the said Sir Roger and Juliana his first wife. And afterwards, a little before the feast of the Nativity of our Lord, in the same fourteenth year, in digging out a fox which was in an earth near Bengebery, the said Margaret was smothered, but not killed on the spot because, after that accident, viz. on Thursday in the feast of the Holy Innocents, in the year of our Lord 1340, she made her will, by permission of the said Sir Roger; and, on the last day of December next following, in the said fourteenth year, died without issue." [General Notices of the Northwoods, - Kent Archaeological Society]

Description and Defences

Binbury was one of the very first motte and bailey types to be rebuilt in stone, the walls being constructed from ragstone and napped flint, around 1.9 meters [8ft] thick. During World War Two the motte was damaged to some degree by the construction of concrete air-raid shelters, and yet it is considered to be a very good example of a man-made motte.

In 2000 a grant of £30,000 was made to stabilise the remaining walls.

Brenchley Castle

A minor structure, near Tonbridge
Postcode for Satnav: TN12 7NS and TN12 7BW
Nearest major road A21

Description and Defences

There is some confusion regarding the Brenchley site. The structure which is known as the castle, at TN12 7BW, is simply a mound of earth, an artificial hill which goes back before Norman times. It may be a burial mound on an Iron Age fortification but unless an excavation were to take place, there simply is nothing there which can provide evidence. A short distance away, at TN12 7NS, there is a private residence which was once a manor house and had crenelated walls and a drawbridge.

There is not a great deal to see nowadays and I would not particularly recommend this site as a place to visit unless you just happen to be passing, or have a particular interest the archaeology of the period.

Bromley Castle

A redeveloped site near Bromley South Railway Station
Postcode for Satnav: BR2 0EN
Nearest major road A232

Also nearby:
Chiselhurst Caves
Horniman Museum
Bethlem Museum of the Mind

This is not the same site as the Bishops Palace which is also covered in this book.

History
The Manor House of Bromley dates back to 1302 when it was fortified by Sir John de Banquel. The building was a ruin by the Tudor period and was demolished in 1869.

Description
Some mounds can be found in Bromley Park between Church Road and Ethelbert Road, but there is nothing structural to see and I would not particularly recommend this site as a place to visit unless you just happen to be passing.

Bromley Palace

A major structure in Bromley Kent
Owned by the local council but with gardens open to the public.
Postcode for Satnav: BR1 3UH
Nearest major road   A21

History

A manor house had existed at Bromley from as early as 862 A.D. and was the property of the church. It had a Holy Well, which had probably been a pagan shrine, and later an oratory, which was a kind of small chapel, where a priest would be paid to say prayers for the soul of a rich person or family. This then became a site of pilgrimage for medieval Christians.

Such establishments became less popular after the protestant reformation and the land was sold off by order of the Parliamentary government in 1648 then returned to the church in 1660 when King Charles II was restored to the throne. The buildings were repaired several times but in 1774 the whole structure was pulled down and rebuilt on the orders of John Thomas, the Bishop of Rochester.

Bromley Palace c1756 [Hastead's History of Kent]

In 1845 the 18th century building was sold off to a wealthy local gentleman named Coles Child. In the 1920s it was a school, and in 1935 it became Stockwell College of Education, for the training of schoolteachers, which closed in 1980. Then in 1982 the local council decided to move their headquarters to the palace buildings.

Bruce W. Johnson

Description

Now serving as part of the Bromley Council Civic Centre, the palace still maintains some signs of its previous grandeur. Inside there is a magnificent grand staircase, carved oak panels, a Robert Adams fireplace, the Mayor's parlour and the Council's Cabinet room.

The building as it now exists is surrounded by some nice green areas and a lake which were all part of the original palace park. There are several interesting features in the park, including St Blaise's Well, the Pulham Rocks, the Ice House, the Ha Ha Wall and a Victorian folly.

There had been a natural water spring on the estate since ancient times. The water contains slight traces of iron and some people claimed that it had health-giving properties. Frequently such wells had played a part in pagan religion, with people making votive offerings, throwing in coins and other gifts to the spirits beneath the earth. The early church tried to blot out these old beliefs by naming such wells after Christian saints. In mediaeval times pilgrims actually came to the well and there was an oratory, where prayers were said to St. Blaise, the patron saint of the wool trade. The chapel was closed down in the reformation.

In 1756 a surgeon called Thomas Reynolds analysed the mineral content of the water and claimed that it contained more minerals than the water from Tonbridge Wells, leading to a resurgence in its popularity. The area around the well is now a decorative rockery or grotto, described as "Pulhamite" as it is constructed from a kind of artificial rock invented by James Pulham, [1820 - 1898]

The Ice House was constructed in the 18th Century from hand-made red bricks. It is partly contained within an earthen bank, and as its name suggests it was used to store large quantities of ice and other perishables. It had cavity walls to provide insulation, one of the earliest examples I know of this technique.

Later, in the 19th Century, ice could be kept in refrigerators and so the building was modified by having a summerhouse built on to the south side, and presumably became a place where visitors could shelter from the heat of the summer. The floors of the building were concreted in the 20th Century.

The Ha-Ha Wall is simply a decorative feature, achieved by laying bricks both horizontally and vertically, to create a kind of basket-weave pattern.

The Victorian folly stands just outside what is now the south west gateway into the civic centre complex. It is a brick turret with a round-arched window in Norman style and some zig-zag decoration. It is believed that some parts of the structure are genuine medieval remnants.

At the time of writing [2022] the Civic Centre was available as a wedding venue with four different suites on offer. The surrounding buildings and the external views of the palace are ideal for wedding photography.

Canterbury Castle

A major structure in Canterbury, owned by the local authority
Postcode for Satnav: CT1 2PR
Nearest major road   A2
Parking Arrangements:
24 hour parking is available immediately across the road from the castle and is ideal for all Canterbury attractions.

Also nearby:
The Simmons Memorial in Dane John Gardens
Medieval City Walls
Roman Museum
Historic Butter market
Canterbury Cathedral.
Historic High Street
Ducking Stool
Medieval Hospital of St Thomas the Martyr
Kent Museum of Freemasonry
Medieval West Gate including Museum

It is perfectly possible to spend the entire day in Canterbury. The castle itself may not take up much time, but the Cathedral, the City Walls, the West Gate, the main streets and the possibility of a boat trip all offer additional opportunities. Make sure you have bought sufficient time on your car parking ticket.

History
Canterbury, like Rochester, commands the road running from London to Dover. It therefore had immense strategic value in the years just after the Norman Conquest and a wooden castle was built immediately. Within fourteen years this was replaced by a stone castle, one of the earliest in the country.

The castle itself was rebuilt in stone between 1086 and 1120 close to the Roman Gate which was known as the Worthgate. It filled a large space where the car park and the Dane John gardens are now.

It was the official headquarters for the sheriff of Kent and his troops who kept law and order on behalf of the king, although usually the sheriff was a nobleman who would have had his own castle somewhere in the county as well.

In the late 1300s there was a period of civil unrest, when members of the lower classes began to follow such groups as the Lollards, who demanded, amongst other things, that the bible should be translated into English. At one point Archbishop Sudbury was murdered by an angry mob! As a consequence the castle and the city walls were repaired, and houses which had been built leaning against the city walls were torn down.

In the 12th century it became a prison and had a bad reputation with local people as a place of suffering and ill treatment. Nevertheless it remained in use until 1609, when King James I gave it to Sir Anthony Weldon. Like many gentlemen of the Tudor and Stuart period, he tore down much of his historic buildings to reuse the building materials. In 1817 there was even an attempt to demolish the keep for this reason, but fortunately there was too much work involved and a large part of the keep was allowed to survive, though the rest of the castle was already gone by then.

Canterbury Castle

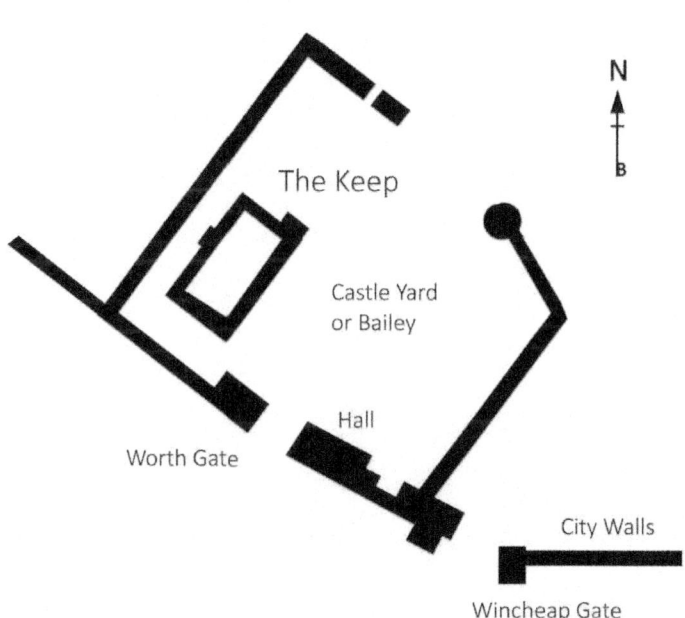

After 1825 the keep was used by a company which sold coal, to store their equipment, leading to the demolition of the internal walls.

In 1928 the castle site was bought by the local city council and preserved as a leisure facility. For many years it was possible to walk inside. At the time of writing, [2022] the keep is closed due to the risk of falling masonry. It can still be seen perfectly clearly, but only from outside the fence. There is, however, a small model of what the castle once looked like.

Description and Defences

The large bailey yard was surrounded by a curtain wall and a deep ditch. The part which still remains is the keep, which was 80 feet high, the third largest keep in England after Dover and Rochester. It is noticeable that it is built with small pieces of flint, because the local stone available in Kent is chalk, which is so soft that it could easily be hacked away by engineers in a siege. Flints are hard, but being so small they require a lot more mortar. When the castle was new these walls would have had an outer layer of good quality stone to give protection against both attackers and the weather.

The entrance to the keep would have been at first floor level. This is a defensive feature. Anyone trying to batter down the doors would have had to somehow get their battering ram up a steep flight of stairs and round a corner, an impossible task, especially when being pelted with rocks by the defenders from the top of the walls.

Bruce W. Johnson

The City of Canterbury and its defences

On the eastern side of the car park a steeple can be seen rising up from the top of a large earth mound. There is a local tradition that it was used by the Normans as the base for a wooden motte and bailey castle and was therefore known as the "donjon" mound which later became corrupted to "Dane John." Sadly this is probably untrue, it seems more likely that the mound was an ancient burial site, going back at least to Roman times and possibly well before.

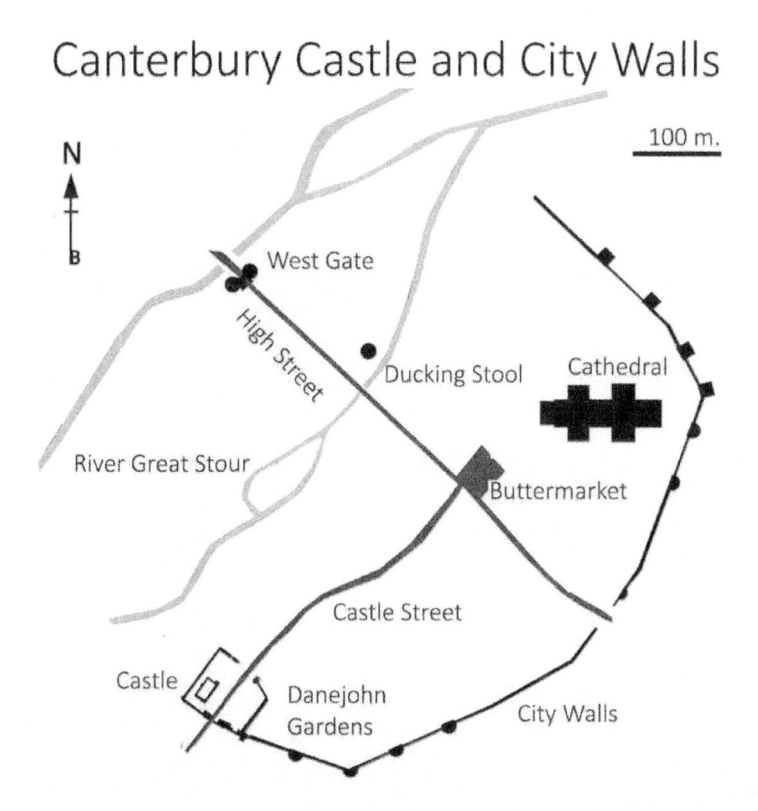

Canterbury Castle and City Walls

Between 1790 and 1803 the grounds around the mound were adopted and reorganised by the local council, with generous financial support from Alderman Simmons, to whom a memorial now stands on top of the mound.

The Dane John Gardens are also an excellent place to see the remaining section of the historic city walls, which are mainly Roman, built in the 3rd Century when attacks from German tribes were already beginning to become a problem.

The walls were repaired in the 14th century [see above] and strengthened with 21 towers. The south and east sides of the city, starting at Dane John Gardens, are the best place to see the walls, including 9 of the towers which are still standing.

There were originally 6 gates to the city, Newgate, Riding Gate, Burgate, Wincheap Gate and Worth Gate as well as the city's West Gate which dates from 1380. One of the city gates, the Wincheap Gate, used to lead straight into the castle yard, or "Bailey," where the road to the parking site now comes off the roundabout.

The West Gate, Canterbury

The Worth Gate was close by enabling ordinary people to pass in and out of the city without passing through the castle. The West Gate is a very high quality example of a city gate, and originally had machicolations, and a drawbridge. It still remains and is in excellent condition. Almost certainly the

"Canterbury Pilgrims" described by Chaucer would have passed through this exact gate. It was used as a prison from Tudor times onwards and in recent times has housed a tiny, but fascinating, museum.

The gothic cathedral is certainly worth visiting, being rich in history. The Archbishop of Canterbury is the supreme cleric of the Church of England, which makes Canterbury Cathedral a religious centre of immense importance.

In 1170 Archbishop Thomas Becket was killed inside the cathedral by a group of knights who believed that they were carrying out the wishes of King Henry II. It is possible to stand on the exact spot where the murder took place in the Cathedral.

Becket became a martyr and Canterbury became the most important place of pilgrimage in medieval Britain, with up to 100,000 visitors a year. When the tomb was destroyed during the reformation, the king's men needed seven large farm carts to carry away all the treasure which had been offered by pilgrims over the years. The cathedral also contains some of the oldest stained glass windows in the country and the tomb of the Black Prince who fought at the Battle of Agincourt.

Castle Rough

A minor structure on private land near Sittingbourne
Postcode for Satnav: ME10 2TU
Nearest major road A2

There is little to see now except some earthworks, ridges and dips in the earth. I would not particularly recommend this site as a place to visit unless you just happen to be passing, or have a particular interest the archaeology of the period.

Description and Defences
The site is a square enclosure fed by a stream which is a tributary of Milton Creek. Local rumours have connected it to the Danes, but the only remains found in an archaeological dig related to the 13th or 14th centuries.

Bruce W. Johnson

Castle Toll

A minor structure, on privately owned farmland near Newenden.
Postcode for Satnav: TN18 5PY
Nearest major road: A28
Parking arrangements: Park in the village and walk

All that remains of the castle are its earthworks, lines of ridges and dips in the ground. These are impressive and significant in the eyes of historians and archaeologists but there are none of the stone structures which the public generally associate with castles. A pleasant walk on a fine day.

History

Originally, the site was probably a prehistoric settlement, but became the Manor of Newenden in the Norman period. It is believed that Edward I used to hunt in the area after 1272, when the manor belonged to Sir Ralph de Seyntleger.

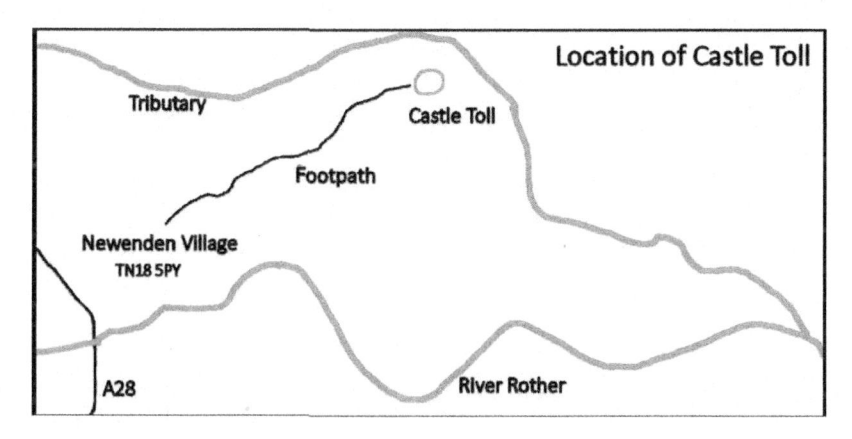

Description and Defences

The actual site has no road access and no post-code but can be found near a footpath, a mile or more to the east of Newenden, on the extreme north-east corner of the parish boundary. It shows up well in aerial photographs of the area. Look for a semi-circle of trees in a ploughed field. That is the actual Castle. Running back from there, towards Newenden the fields are the north-western side of what was once a large triangular earthwork, enclosing at least 18 acres of land. The eastern side follows a tributary to the River Rother and the southern boundary is the river itself.

Chiddingstone Castle

A major structure near Tonbridge. National Trust
Postcode for Satnav: TN8 7AH
Nearest major road   A21
Websites:
https://www.chiddingstonecastle.org.uk/
https://www.nationaltrust.org.uk/chiddingstone-village
Parking Arrangements:
At the time of writing it was possible to park freely along the Chiddingstone Road leading out of the village.

Also nearby
Chiddingstone village
Church of St. Mary the Virgin
The actual "Chidding Stone."

Chiddingstone is an almost perfect spot for cyclists and hikers to take a break on a summer's day. Although the street is owned by the National Trust, there is no entry fee for visiting the village which has a pub, a post office and cafes and gift shops. Don't be afraid to look up the alleyways leading to the cafe.

I would advise visitors to check opening dates and times of the castle as it is not open during winter months. The grounds are open and look beautiful when the spring bulbs are out. Full details can be found on the website.

History
Chiddingstone Castle is a Mock Gothic creation, and important in its own right for that reason. The nineteenth century is famous for what was known as "The Romantic Movement." Society had become less religious during the Enlightenment but by Victorian times many people sought to find alternative sources of spiritual pleasure in art, architecture and literature, particularly those styles which appealed to the romance and chivalry of the Middle Ages. Chiddingstone Castle reflects that period of fascination with the romantic past.

The Streatfield family were originally from Estreville in Normandy and were the Lords of the Manor throughout most of the last thousand years.

An earlier manor house did exist on the site but was demolished in 1679 and replaced with a red-brick mansion, a style which was very fashionable in the Restoration Period, possibly due to the Dutch influences of the time.

In 1808 the house belonged to Henry Streatfield, the High Sheriff of Kent, who had the walls refaced with natural stone to hide the red-brick, and also added a variety of Gothic features especially fortifications All of this was seen as very trendy at the time. Further Gothic features were added in the 19th Century when the house passed to Sir Henry's son, another Henry. Under his direction, long, Gothic style lancet windows were added together with a gatehouse, which again had the look of a real castle, but simply no enemy knights to defend against. The building was used as a school after 1936, as well as being used by the British Armed Forces during World War Two.

From 1955 onwards the castle became a home again, under the ownership of Mr. Denys Eyre Bower, a wealthy collector of antiques, with several collections including Japanese Stuart and Jacobite, Buddhist, and Ancient Egyptian exhibits, of which the Japanese collection is particularly rich and varied, including exquisite lacquered furniture and Japanese swords.

The castle gardens are extremely pleasant, with a lake, caves, natural rock formations and a river crossed by a wooden bridge. I recently visited in March when there was an excellent display of spring bulbs in bloom. At the time of writing [2022] the castle was available as a high quality wedding venue.

Chiddingstone Village

Chiddingstone Village

Chiddingstone village is directly adjacent to the castle, with just a pleasant five minute walk between them. It is a traditional one-street village, which was a common arrangement before the agricultural revolution, when population increased and towns grew larger.

The settlement is unique in as much as it is entirely owned by the National Trust, which describes it as "the best example of a Tudor village left in the country". Although small, it is extremely pretty, and provides a perfect background for a holiday snap to send your friends!

The Church of St Mary the Virgin

Also in the village stands the Church of St. Mary the Virgin, a large parish church, especially considering the size of the village. It was almost destroyed by fire, following a lightning strike in 1624. Fortunately it survived as it is a beautiful building, generally open to visitors, and well worth a visit.

Among the many interesting and attractive features in the church there are several plaques and stained glass windows which bear the Streatfield family motto "Data Fata Secutus." This can be translated as "Fortune follows fate" or "I follow my destiny." Perhaps reflected in a more modern expression, that in life "You have to be play the cards you were dealt."

Out in the churchyard there is a stone gazebo built in 1736 which serves as an entrance to the steps leading down into the Streatfield family vault. It is said that the vault is ventilated by air vents located in two false tombs nearby, although I did not notice them on my visit.

In the area nearby there is a large boulder, called the Chiding Stone from which the village takes its name. It has been suggested by some that this served as a location where women who had offended in some way might have been required to stand for several hours as a punishment. Whether there is any truth in this story I cannot say.

Bruce W. Johnson

Chilham Castle

A major structure near Ashford, privately owned, and not open to the public.
Postcode for Satnav: CT4 8DB
Nearest major road   A2 / A28
Website: https://www.chilham-castle.co.uk/
Parking Arrangements: On site. [For official functions]
Public Transport: Chilham Station - 15 minute walk.

Also nearby
Castle Gardens
Chilham Village

There are actually two castles at Chilham, a Norman keep and a Jacobean stately home, as shown in this print by Watts, dated 1785. Both parts are still lived in.

History

The Normans built a wooden motte and bailey castle on the site immediately after the conquest. A "Motte" is a steep mound of earth which the castles stands on top of, as opposed to a "Moat" which is a defensive ditch around the castle.

The present stone keep was then built by Chilham de Lucy in 1174, which accounts for its name.

Bartholomew de Badlesmere was born at Chilham I 1275 and inherited it on his father's death in 1301. His life tells the story of his rise and dramatic fall. It also links this site to other castles such as Dover and Leeds. By 1306 Badlesmere was one of the Members of Parliament for Kent. By 1310 he was the deputy constable of England and in 1314 he fought at Bannockburn. Thus he was seen as a strong supporter of the King and in 1317 he became custodian of Leeds Castle, also in Kent.

King Edward II of England was a rather tragic figure. Believed to be bisexual, he allowed himself to be influenced by "favourites" who were literally robber barons, using their position with the king to make gains through violence and dishonesty. Edward's main opponent was the Duke of Lancaster.

By 1318, Badlesmere had managed to arrange some sort of peace between the two and was rewarded by being made Steward of the King's Household, a post of high status which brought him considerable financial rewards. In 1319 he hosted a great feast for the King at Chilham and in 1320 he was given control over Dover Castle and became Warden of the Cinque Ports. In effect, he had become one of the most powerful men in the King's service. Around this time, however, he began to follow a political path which would ultimately destroy him.

Chilham Castle and Keep, detail from a print by Watts, c1785

In 1321 things turned sour. The conflict between Lancaster and King Edward had become more virulent. Bartholomew de Badlesmere became part of a middle party, who opposed the kings favourites but without the hatred of Lancaster's group. Edward saw this as disloyalty and took back control of Dover Castle.

Meanwhile the Queen went on pilgrimage to Canterbury, and on the way back called in at Leeds Castle [Kent] demanding that she and her guards be allowed to enter. Badlesmere's wife, Margaret De Clare, was commanding the castle. She refused to open the gates and when the Queen's men tried to force their way in, Margaret ordered her archers to shoot, killing six of the royal escort. This, of course had been a trap. To shoot at the Queen's bodyguard was considered an act of rebellion and it provided King Edward with an excuse to attack Leeds Castle and to order the arrest of Bartholomew de Badlesmere. Realising that he was in mortal danger, Badlesmere raised an armed force, but his allies were further north and could not support him. He was tried at Canterbury in April 1322 and sentenced to be hung, drawn and quartered.

That very same day he was dragged for three miles to Blean, where he was hanged until almost dead and then beheaded, his head being put on display on the Burgh Gate at Canterbury. He had many properties in addition to Chilham and most of them were confiscated.

From 1542 Chilham Castle was held by Sir Thomas Cheyney but he effectively demolished most of the old castle and used the materials to construct Shurland Hall, on the Isle of Sheppey. His son sold what was left of the estate to Sir Thomas Kempe but Kempe had no sons of his own to leave it to and one of his daughters married Sir Dudley Digges, an investor, diplomat and Member of Parliament in the period before the English civil war. Digges began work on the new house which was completed in 1616. Although intended as a residence it has deliberately been decorated with many of the features we would associate with traditional castles, such as battlements and corner towers. It also features clusters of red-brick chimneys which were popular in the 16th and early 17th centuries.

Like so many castles and stately homes, Chilham suffered some decay with the passing of the centuries, but in 1918 it was bought by Sir Edmund Davies, who invested in its restoration.

In October 2022 local newspapers carried details of a sale of artworks and memorabilia including both historical artefacts as well as more modern items by the late designer Chrisopher Gibbs.

https://www.kentlive.news/news/property/historic-artefacts-chilham-castle-offered-7569375

Chilham Castle, Norman Keep and Jacobean Mansion.

Description and Defences

The Norman keep is octagonal in shape, with a square stair-turret and a barbican. It stands in a walled courtyard, or inner bailey, which had a well.

It is still used as a residence, making it one of the oldest inhabited buildings in the country.

The castle building is privately owned and is closed to the public but is available as a venue for certain types of events and details are given on their website. The main hall is a spectacular venue for suitable functions. There are also regular equestrian events.

Chilham Castle

[Map showing Bailey Yard, Keep, and Barbican with N/S compass]

The gardens, which stretch towards the river Stour, were designed by John Tradescant the Elder, only to be remodelled by an even more famous landscaper, Capability Brown. At the time of writing, [2022] the gardens are open to the public on two days each week in the summer months. [See website for details].

When closed the castle can be glimpsed through the gates from School Hill, CT4 8DA.

Chilham Village

Chilham is one of the most beautiful villages in England by virtue of its timber framed medieval houses looking out onto a generously sized village square.

The local church, St. Marys of Chilham dates back to the Domesday survey of 1086, and has a tower built in 1534.

At the time of writing [2022] there is also a pub, a post office, tea-rooms and a farm shop in the village.

Coldbridge [Colebridge] Castle

A redeveloped site between Maidstone and Ashford. Privately owned
Postcode for Satnav: TN27 9BP
Nearest major road M20

Coldbridge Farm, 2 miles south of Boughton Malherbe Place, is believed to stand on the site of Colebridge Castle, a fortified manor house.

History

Colebridge was constructed by Fulk de Peyforer in 1314 but quickly passed to the Leybourne family, who enlarged it using an unusual triangular plan for the outer ward. In 1363 Sir Robert Corbye began to build his own fortified dwelling at Boughton Malherbe Place, nearby, and it appears that large parts of Coldbridge were pulled down to be used as building materials. The Leybournes were still living there at the time, so presumably they let the castle walls go and simply used the central building as a house. The land later passed to John, Duke of Lancaster, and then into the hands of the church.

Description

Little now remains of the castle, except some earthworks, which are easily seen in aerial photographs as the thick line of trees on the northern and western sides of the farmhouse. I would not recommend visiting the site unless you live nearby or have a particular interest.

Bruce W. Johnson

Cooling Castle

A major structure near Rochester. Privately owned
Postcode for Satnav: ME3 8DT
Nearest major road   M2/ A2 / A289
Website for wedding receptions: https://www.coolingcastlebarn.com/
Parking Arrangements: on site for wedding guests, otherwise roadside.

Also nearby;
St. Margaret's Church, High Halstow.
RSPB Nature Reserve, High Halstow.

Cooling Castle lies out in a fairly remote part of Kent, known as the Hoo Peninsula. The area is truly rural, with small country villages nestling between farmers' fields full of short apple-trees and hops growing up poles. Your route may take you past St. Margaret's Church, High Halstow, and it is worth stopping there to take in the view down towards the river, where prison hulks were once anchored. It is believed that the churchyard was the setting for an incident in Charles Dickens' book "Great Expectations." A notice board in the church yard gives further information.

On arriving at Cooling Castle, the outer gatehouse and some of the towers can easily be seen from the road. The rest of the castle is private property and not open to the public.

History

Cooling Castle was built in the 1380s by the local lord of the manor, Sir John Cobham, to guard the area against raids by the French and Spanish during the Hundred Years War. It was originally sited on the south bank of thee River Thames, but due to silting up over the centuries it now lies in the middle of the Hoo Peninsula.

In January 1554 the castle was captured and badly damaged by Sir Thomas Wyatt, during his unsuccessful protestant rebellion against Queen Mary Tudor. The Cobhams failed to put up much of a fight, possibly because their troops had gone off to fight the rebels, leaving very few men to defend the place, less than a dozen perhaps. It was captured on the very first day of fighting, which lasted no more than a few hours.

The castle was badly damaged in this assault, due to Wyatt having already captured a number of cannons. Queen Mary, however, suspected that the Cobhams had put little effort into the defence as they were trying to back both sides at the same time. As a result Lord Cobham spent some time as a prisoner in the Tower of London, before he finally got his land back. The

Castles of Kent

castle was subsequently abandoned by the Cobhams and in 1670 the site was returned to use as a farm, by Sir Thomas Whitmore.

Design and Defences

The castle has an unusual layout. Most quadrangular castles would have been constructed on a single moated island.

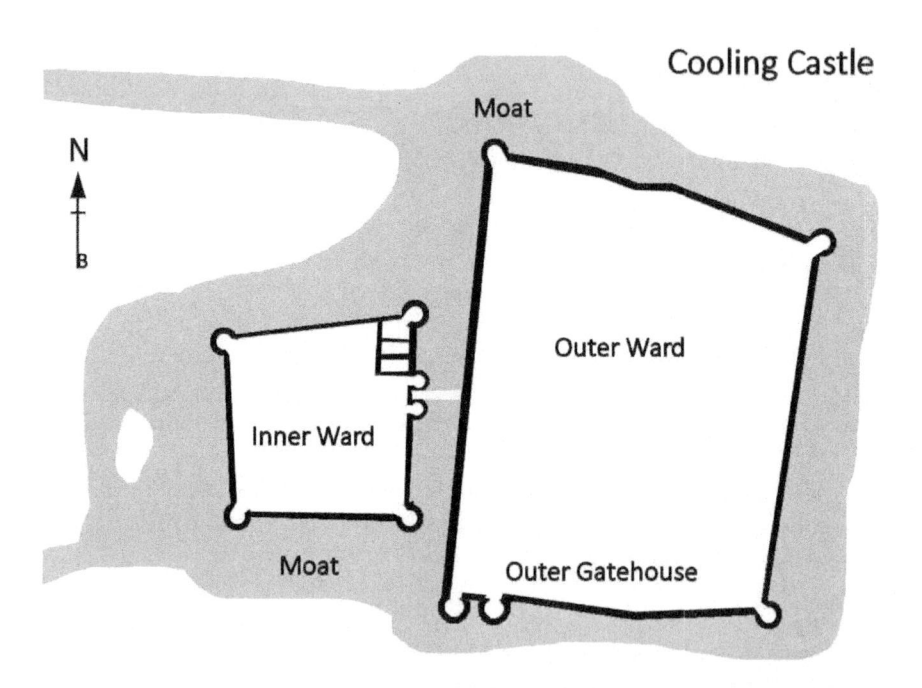

Cooling Castle

Moat

N

Outer Ward

Inner Ward

Moat   Outer Gatehouse

The plan of Cooling Castle [above] corresponds to the 1735 print by Buck [below] showing two sections, each on its own ground.

Cooling had an inner ward, [castle yard] around the castle, then to the west of that, on another island, there was a much larger ward [440 x 290 ft.]

This was probably intended to for local people to shelter from potential raiders. It was completely walled, with horseshoe-shaped towers on the corners, and was accessed via the outer gatehouse at its south-west corner.

Some sections of the curtain wall still remain, including some parts decorated with stone chequer-board patterns, close to the inner gatehouse.

The corner towers protrude about 5 metres (16 ft.) in front of the curtain wall and are still standing to a height of 12 metres (39 ft.) Two of them can be accessed from the roadside, although they are in a very poor state of repair and should be approached with great care.

Cooling Castle: Corner Tower and Moat

The photograph above shows the tower and wall at the south east corner of inner bailey. To the right one can see the remains of the curtain wall of the outer bailey. The flat grassy area between the structures would have been the moat, which is now partly silted up.

The most impressive remaining feature of Cooling is the massive outer gatehouse, with its crenellations and machicolations, at the south-west corner of the outer ward. It has enjoyed protected status as a monument since 1946.

Cooling Castle: The Outer Gatehouse

Bruce W. Johnson

Cooling Castle: Rear view of Gate Towers

The towers of the gatehouse were deliberately left open at the back, so that if an enemy managed to capture one it would provide no protection from defending archers.

This defensive feature is portrayed in Hooper's print of 1784, and is interesting for several reasons. It also illustrates how the castle was no longer used for defence, with a wooden shed in the castle yard and a simple five-bar gate being used in the archway. In fact, the towers in the picture appear to be in use as agricultural silos, for the stacking of hay.

Cooling Castle: Detail from a print by Hooper, c1748

Defensive Features

Cooling may possibly have been the first English castle designed for the age of gunpowder weapons. There are portholes for guns as well as arrow slits and it utilises moats and ditches which would remain effective even when walls had been shot down.

Cooling Castle: Gun Port

The towers also provide us with a superb example of what are called "Machicolations"

These are openings beneath the battlements through which the defenders could drop stones or incendiary materials onto attackers.

Cooling Castle: Machicolations

Castles of Kent

High up on the right-hand tower there is a copper plaque with an inscription. Members of the Kent Archaeological Society visited the castle in 1863 and again in 1864, using ladders to examine the plate at close quarters. In 1866 a Mr Waller published a report of their findings. Some parts of the plaque had actually fallen off and had been retrieved from the moat and fixed back in position. Unfortunately they had been fixed back in place with iron nails, causing the copper to corrode!

The plaque reads:

Knouwyth that beth and schul be
That I am mad in help of the cuntre
In knowing of whyche thing
Thys is chartre and wytnessyng

In modern English this means;

Know [those] that are [now living] and shall be [living]
That I am made to help the country
In knowing of which thing
This is [a] charter and witnessing.
It was probably intended to reassure the local public that the castle was not going to be used to enforce any kind of tyranny.

At the time of writing [2022] part of the outer bailey is in use as a wedding venue comprising a large historic barn, used for receptions and also accommodation for guests to stay overnight. See the Cooling Barn website for details. [Details above.]

The remainder of the castle is now used as a private house and garden.

Bruce W. Johnson

Deal Castle

A major structure in Deal. English Heritage
Postcode for Satnav: CT14 7BA
Nearest major road A2 / A256
Website: https://www.english-heritage.org.uk/visit/places/deal-castle/
Parking Arrangements: Pay and display car park. Free for members of English Heritage.
Public transport: Regular bus and trains to Deal Station [½ a mile]

Also nearby:
The Captain's Garden, Victoria Road CT14 7AY
Deal Pleasure Pier: Opened by the Duke of Edinburgh in 1957, 313 meters long and featuring a cafe, bar, lounge, and fishing decks CT14 6HY
Deal Timeball Tower: A small museum which was once a semaphore station. CT14 7BP
Walmer Castle and Gardens are within walking distance, about one mile.

Visiting Deal Castle is a unique experience, combining a historical adventure with all the attractions of a day at the seaside.

History

King Henry VIII reigned over England from 1509 to 1547. During the 1530s he had broken away from the Roman Catholic Church and married Anne Boleyn. By 1538, he was in fear of an invasion, by one of the great Catholic powers, either France or Spain. He therefore began the construction of a string of coastal fortresses. Many of these have disappeared, either demolished or washed away by the sea. Of those which remain, Deal is absolutely the showpiece.

It may seem strange, but three of the castles, at Sandown, Walmer and Deal were all built within a mile of each other, overlooking the Goodwin Sands, and were interconnected by earthwork fortifications. This part of the coast, known as the Downs, was a sheltered area for ships to anchor and it must have been seen as an obvious place for an invading force to land.

All three castles were built within two years, and were designed on a geometrical plan, similar to European forts being designed by Albrecht Durer at that time. Unlike medieval castles, these Tudor forts were deliberately built with deep ditches and low walls, to present less of a target for ship's cannon-balls, evidence that military architecture was evolving in response to advances in the technology of war.

On 27 December 1539, Anne of Cleves, Henry VIII's new wife-to-be, landed at Deal and rested at the castle before continuing on her journey to meet the king, even though the building work was unfinished at the time.

As students of history may be aware, Henry had been taken in by a rather flattering portrait, but when they actually met, the king was not entirely taken with his new bride, whom he described as a "Fat Flanders Mare."

Deal Castle, from a print by Daniel, c1823

From the beginning, Deal Castle came under the overall command of the Lord Warden of the Cinque Ports, who in turn appointed a captain. The captain was responsible for maintaining the castle, its garrison, guns and stores. He also led the garrison in wartime. In fact, Henry's forts were never tested against invaders, and saw no action until the following century. In 1639, the Battle of the Downs, a naval battle between the Spanish and the Dutch, took place in the English Channel in sight of Deal Castle. Several Spanish vessels were sunk and 2,000 shipwrecked sailors came ashore at Deal and Dover.

The English Civil War broke out in 1642. The south-east of England was firmly on the side of Parliament, especially the City of London, where the merchant class opposed King Charles I for both his taxation policies and his religious doctrines. Having won the war, by 1645, the parliamentary side then became less popular, and in 1648 a series of rebellions broke out across Britain, generally referred to as the Second Civil War. The fleet, which was anchored off the Downs, mutinied against Parliament and took possession of the three castles. The revolt was unsuccessful and the castles were recaptured by Colonel Nathaniel Rich, with a fairly small force of 2000 men and a few cannons.

After the English Civil War the castles were kept in good repair as defences against the Dutch and the French.

Description and Defences

The outer defence of Deal Castle is a dry moat. The entire castle sits inside this, so that most of the outer walls are beneath ground level and therefore well protected from artillery fire.

The main defences consist of six circular bastions arranged on a sex-foil plan. Six smaller circles, form the next level, and in the centre there is a keep which serves as a watchtower as well as providing an internal connection between all of the floors. All of these levels could hold cannon, with the higher ones firing over the lower ones so that the entire firepower of the fort could be brought into play at the same time.

Within the defences, the castle is very atmospheric, especially "the Rounds" which are underground passageways snaking right round the bottom of the outer defences. The walls are well provided with embrasures, small holes suitable for shooting out of, and it should be noted that some of these are down at the lowest level, enabling the defenders to fire on any attackers who had managed to get down into the moat.

Deal Castle

Dover Castle

A major structure in Dover. English Heritage
Postcode for Satnav: CT16 1HU
Nearest major road A2
[Please note the traffic information at the end of the Dover section]
Website:
https://www.english-heritage.org.uk/visit/places/dover-castle/
Parking Arrangements: Free parking for up to 200 cars
Public transport: South-eastern Trains to Dover Priory also local buses.

Also nearby
Knights Templar Church [Remains] CT17 9DP
Western Heights of Dover, fortress [English Heritage] CT17 9DZ
[There is no access to the inside, only the moat]
South Foreland Lighthouse [National Trust] CT15 5NA [2 miles]
Fan Bay Deep Shelter [National Trust] CT15 6HP [1 mile]
Dover Museum and Bronze Age Boat Gallery CT16 1PH
Bleriot Memorial: CT16 1HW
Fort Burgoyne CT15 5LP

History

Dover Castle was designed to impress, as a warning to foreign enemies that if they ever dared to invade the shores of England, then they would be met with solid resistance. In this modern age it remains impressive, both for its sheer massive proportions and because it has survived in such excellent condition.

Before the Romans arrived there was already an Iron Age hill fort on the cliff tops. The Romans built the Pharos, a Roman lighthouse, to guide their ships into the harbour safely. That structure still exists inside the castle grounds. Later a fort may have been built beneath the cliffs to protect the port.

When the Romans left a substantial Saxon township grew up on the clifftops, making use of the old Iron Age earthworks for defence. These buildings had been upgraded to a timber castle by 1050 and in the years just before the Norman Conquest, King Harold gave orders for its defences to be strengthened.

After the Norman Conquest, Dover Castle was eventually rebuilt in stone. The powerful castle which we see today really emerged between 1180 and 1200 AD., when King Henry II ordered the construction of a massive keep and curtain wall. It is classed as a "Concentric castle." The keep is surrounded by the inner walls, and these in turn are surrounded by the outer walls which reach out as far as the clifftops, to deny an attacker any space on that side.

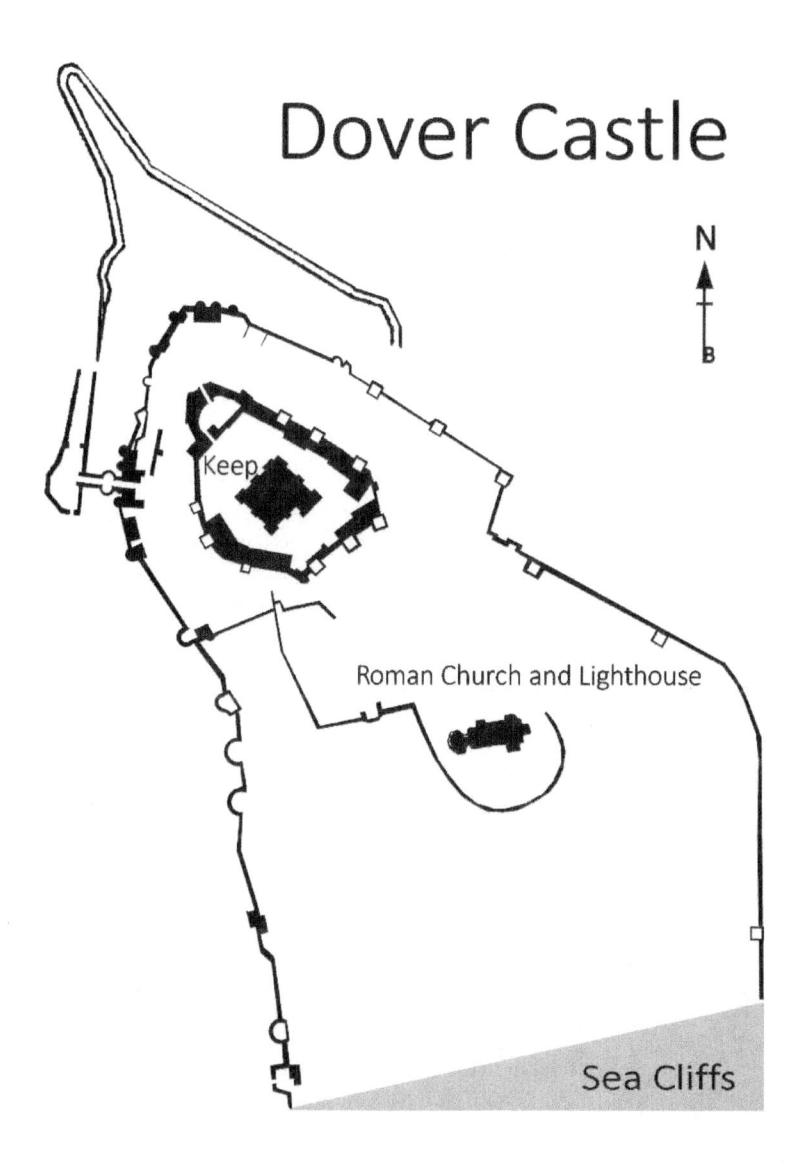

Dover Castle

Keep

Roman Church and Lighthouse

Sea Cliffs

The outer bailey

The outer bailey is basically a large yard, which protected all those things which the castle would need, such as workshops, storehouses, stables and farm animals for food. It is defended by a wall which goes all the way round, shielding everything, and is therefore described as a curtain wall. The towers are square, which helps us to date the whole structure. Square towers were used just after the Norman Conquest. Later buildings had round towers which were stronger for the simple reason that there were no corners to be knocked off.

Inner curtain wall with square towers

The inner bailey is protected by another huge curtain wall complete with fourteen square towers. In the medieval period the walls would have been lined with timber framed buildings such as barracks, workshops and store-rooms. The gateways through the curtain wall have their own defensive towers. One noteworthy defence feature is that these towers were often built with open backs. This was deliberate, so that if a tower was captured it provided no cover for the enemy troops.

The Keep

The entrance to the keep was protected by its own fore-castle. Potential attackers would have to fight their way into this sturdy building and would then need to struggle up a narrow internal stairway which turned a corner before coming to the small drawbridge which led to the main door of the keep. Getting a battering ram, or even a ladder up the stairway would have been virtually impossible. The top floor of the gatehouse was used, in peace time, as a chapel.

In a medieval castle the keep had two main functions. In the event of a siege the keep would become the last bastion of defence, with walls which were tall enough and strong enough to hold back the attackers for as long as possible. In peace time it served as the headquarters building. The upper stories were often the living accommodation for the commander and his family, whilst the lower storeys were given over to store-rooms, kitchens and perhaps a dungeon. The bottom floor of the keep was a storage area and had a baker's oven. The rest of the keep is divided into two halves by a cross-wall. This feature was also used elsewhere, and it prolonged the siege of Rochester by some time, with King John's men in control of one half but his enemies still in possession of the other side.

At Dover we can see one obvious sign that preparations had been made for the mundane aspects of everyday life, in that all of the main chambers had their own private toilets, which in those days were called "Garde-Robes," because they didn't usually have fitted doors, so it was customary to hang one's coat across the doorway as the only way of ensuring privacy.

Two of the corner towers contain spiral staircases which lead all the way up to the roof, offering splendid views out over the English Channel.

At the time of writing, [2022] a real effort has been made by the castle management and staff to provide a rich reconstruction of the historical environment inside Dover Keep.

This basic design, of a central keep surrounded by encircling walls, is known as a "Concentric Castle" or a "Curtain Wall Castle." It became a classic style of the Middle-Ages, but few if any could compete with Dover for sheer size. Henry's two sons, Richard the Lionheart and his brother John both spent heavily on improving the castle further in view of their conflicts with the French Kings of the period.

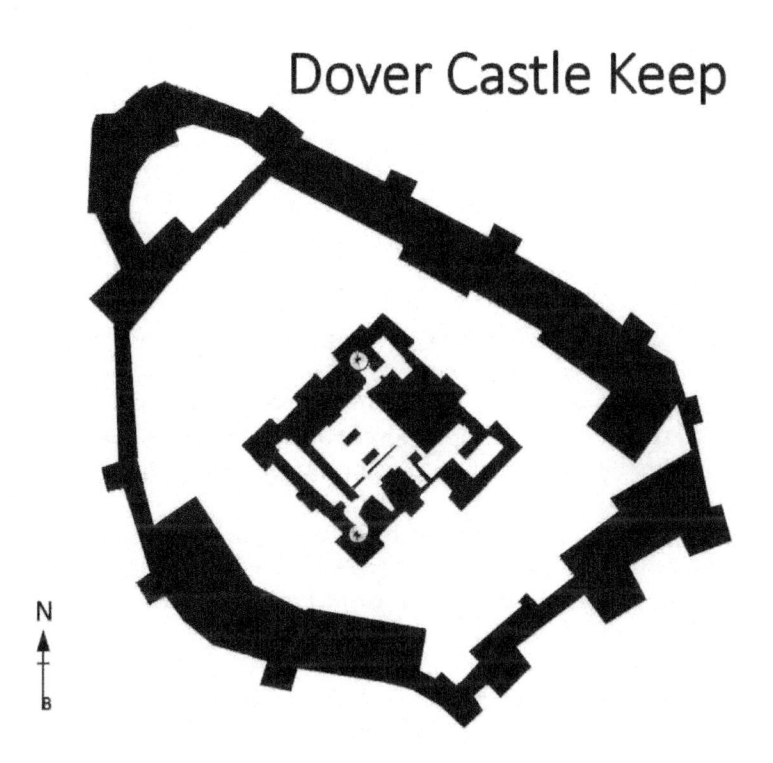

Dover Castle Keep

John is believed to have added additional walls on the north side as well as extra towers, which are 'D' shaped, as opposed to the square towers erected by his father. There was also a large gate-house at the northern tip of the castle enclosure, with its two flanking towers built to a very high standard and connected to one another by underground tunnels.

All of these works were put to the test in 1216. King John had already lost some of his French lands to King Philip Augustus. At home he was having difficulties with the rebel Barons who had forced him to sign the Magna Carta but were soon at war with him again. At their invitation, Prince Louis of France, the son of Philip Augustus, landed in England with a French army on 21st May 1216. He quickly captured Canterbury and Rochester, entering London in triumph on the 2nd of June.

Louis then marched west to capture Winchester, while King Alexander of Scotland and the Welsh prince Llewelyn, rushed to pledge their support. Winchester and London were the two greatest cities in England, and having captured them Louis turned his attention to Dover Castle, which, obviously, was of great strategic importance for a French army, and was famously described by the chronicler, Matthew Paris as "Clavis Angliae", "The Key to England."

Obviously it was easier for the French to attack from the north, the inland side, rather than climbing up the cliffs. A medieval book entitled "Histoire des Ducs de Normandie et des Rois d'Angleterre." contains a detailed report of the siege and gives us good reason to believe that the defences on that side, built by Richard and John, were absolutely state of the art, including a great gatehouse with twin drum towers either side of the gateway, connected by underground tunnels.

The Constable of the castle was Hubert de Burgh, the Earl of Kent and Justiciar of England. He was a veteran soldier and a loyal supporter of King John. He also had a good sized garrison, which is more relevant than we might imagine. In peace time a castle might have a garrison of only a dozen men, and some were easily captured when wars broke out. Dover was well manned, with 140 knights and a larger number of ordinary soldier, men at arms.

Outside the castle, over the ditch from the gatehouse, on the north side there was a barbican of earth and timber. It was undermined by engineers with a siege engine, and the French rushed in but were beaten and pushed back. This was the first actual attack of the siege, but at this point King John died, leaving his crown to his nine year old son, Henry III. Many of the Barons, who had opposed King John, now took the opportunity to switch their alliances to the new boy king. That gave them an opportunity to gain power and be forgiven of any charges of treason.

Prince Louis marched off to besiege London, perhaps hoping to control the succession, but as the barons turned against him his power was slipping and controlling Dover became ever more important. Half of his army went off to campaign further north and Louis returned to Dover three months later and took up his siege where he had left off. This time he began using a very large catapult called a trebuchet but the walls were strong enough to resist it. The French then dug tunnels underneath one of the towers on the gatehouse, propping up the tunnels with timber. When they had dug out a large enough area beneath the gatehouse tower they set the timbers on fire to cause a collapse.

Although he may have damaged the gatehouse, Louis never actually captured the castle itself. He had divided his forces, and half of his army was destroyed at the battle of Lincoln on 20th May 1217. Then the fleet carrying French reinforcements was beaten by the British navy at the battle of Sandwich, forcing Louis to seek peace.

However, by 1264 the English Barons were again in revolt, led by Simon de Montfort. For a while Simon had the upper hand and even imprisoned the heir to the throne, Prince Edward. Things turned bad for the rebels when Simon de Montfort was killed in battle and Prince Edward escaped from captivity. When the royal armies besieged Dover Castle it was Simon's widow, Eleanor de Montfort who commanded the defence of the castle, until such times as she could negotiate a deal to leave the country and have her supporters pardoned.

The new king of England, Henry III, improved the castle further, including the blocking up of earlier gateways and the construction of the Constable's Gateway, an exceptionally strong military structure built between 1279 and 1288. It takes its name from the fact that the private residence of the constable was in the rooms above the entrance, rather than the main keep. All of the rest of the castle is inside the curtain wall.

Two hundred years later, Henry VIII had loopholes made in the walls for cannons to fire through. The castle then survived virtually unaltered until the Napoleonic era when further modifications were made. The towers and the walls were reduced in height, and had earth piled up in front of them, all to ensure that they would be a less vulnerable target for modern cannons.

During the Second World War the castle was still considered a key part in England's defences, both as a strongpoint controlling the harbour and as a headquarters building. It remains a symbol of national pride.

The underground tunnels

During the siege of 1216 the French dug tunnels under the northern gate, in an effort to collapse it. The normal way to prevent this was for the defenders to dig their own tunnels and intercept the incoming ones. These tunnels were extended in medieval times, perhaps as a kind of escape route if needed. In the Napoleonic era they were enlarged as part of the defences, and trap doors were added. There is a system of guided tours to the tunnels, the visit taking almost an hour.

They were still in use during the Second World War and would have been useful as shelter from German bombing raids. Extra tunnels were built to accommodate an underground hospital, known as the annexe level. This facility is open to visitors, but don't expect any treatment! Access is by a 20 minute guided tour which is included in the admission price.

Operation Dynamo

In 1940 more than 300,000 British and allied troops were trapped by the German Armies, with their backs to the sea around the port of Dunkirk.

Castles of Kent

Working from a secret base in the underground tunnels, Vice-Admiral Bertram Ramsay masterminded the planning of Operation Dynamo, sending a fleet of ships, both large and small, to rescue the soldiers from the beaches. There is now an excellent exhibition commemorating this incredible mission, one of the legends of British military history.

Dover Castle stands as a symbol of national independence, defying invaders for a thousand years. Such was the importance of the castle that since 1267 the Constable of Dover has also carried the title of Lord Warden of the Cinque Ports. These were the towns and castles along the coast which were intended to defend the coastline from the French. The titles still remain but are now really only ceremonial honours. From 1978 to 2002 the posts were held by Queen Elizabeth, the Queen Mother.

Other things to see inside the castle grounds

The castle site has been in for more than two thousand years and there are several other attractions within the castle grounds, including a genuine Roman lighthouse and a Saxon Church. Modern attractions include the "Fire Command Post" dating from the First World War, from where observers could monitor shipping in the channel and even fire the earliest anti-aircraft guns at German Zeppelin airships. There are also several gun batteries from the Second World War.

A military museum stands on the eastern side of the bailey yard. The Princess of Wales' Royal Regiment & Queens Regiment Museum houses a display of several interesting collections which preserve the history and traditions of as many as 12 earlier regiments reaching back more than 400 years. One item has a particular poignancy for me, and that is the actual leather football which some of the British troops kicked along in front of them as they advanced across no-man's land on the first day of the Battle of the Somme in 1916.

Important traffic information

Dover is easily reached by either the A2/M2 or the M20, however, from time to time, there may be traffic delays on these roads caused by problems at the channel crossing. If you are aware of delays the following alternative directions may be worth bearing in mind;

If there are delays on the A2: Turn off at Whitfield CT16 2ET, and follow the A256 towards the castle, CT16 1HU

If travelling by the M20/A20 you may experience heavy traffic at times of transport disruption, in which case you may prefer to leave the motorway and follow one of the following routes;

Bruce W. Johnson

Turn off at Alkham Valley towards CT15 7EW and continue along Alkham Valley Road to Kearsney Abbey Gardens [CT16 3DZ], then follow the A256 and Connaught Road towards the castle, CT16 1HU

OR

Turn off at the Court Wood Interchange. This provides the opportunity to stop for a quick look at Abbots Cliff Sound Mirror [CT18 7HZ] an old fashioned invention with a view out to sea. Then take Folkestone Road, B2011, passing by the Premiere Inn [CT15 7EB] and continue along Folkestone Road to join the A256 just after Dover Priory Railway Station, and continue towards the castle, CT16 1HU

Dymchurch Redoubt

A major structure near Hythe. Ministry of defence: Not open to public
Postcode for Satnav: DA4 0AA
Nearest major road: A259

Built in the Napoleonic Wars, Dymchurch redoubt was intended as a headquarters and supply depot for the network of Martello towers. The actual building measures 68 meters wide, 12 m high and surrounded by a dry moat. Its defences were built to hold ten 24 pounder guns, which would be too big and heavy for use on a normal battlefield, but were capable of damaging a ship off shore. They would have stood on platforms which could be turned to face the target.

The redoubt was never attacked by Napoleon, but was brought back into defence during the two world wars, and has been used in more modern times to train British troops for urban warfare on the streets of Northern Ireland.

Safety Warning
The surrounding area is still used as a firing range. In particular, stay clear when red flags are flying.

Bruce W. Johnson

Eastwell Manor

A major structure near Ashford. Privately owned and operated as a hotel
Postcode for Satnav: TN25 4HR
Nearest major road: M20
Website: https://www.champneys.com/hotels/eastwell-manor/
Parking Arrangements: Car park for guests
Public transport: Ashford railway station [not walking distance]

Also nearby:
Godinton House and Gardens
Port Lympne Safari Park
Chilham Castle
Chilham village and village hall.

Eastwell Manor seen through the main entrance.

Eastwell Manor is really a fortified manor house, rather than a true castle, but I have included it here because it is currently in service as a luxury spa hotel, and therefore useful to readers who wish to stay in places with historical character. Eastwell Manor certainly has plenty of that, and some of the biggest fireplaces I have seen in any castle or stately home.

There are records of a manor on these lands going back to Anglo-Saxon times, with a natural spring which became known as the "East Well."

The house as we see it today was built between 1540 and 1550 as a residence for Sir Thomas Moyle, the MP for Rochester who had acted as one of Henry VIII's commissioners during the abolition of the monasteries. The manor house was characterised by a spacious stone-flagged courtyard, massive fireplaces and a crenelated outer wall. However, the building was enlarged and refurbished in the 1790s by George Finch-Hatton, 9th Earl of Winchelsea. Fortunately, he chose to stick with the original Tudor style.

His grandson, the 11th Earl, had to leave the property due to financial difficulties and it was let out to the Duke of Abercorn for five years. The manor reached the peak of its importance in the Victorian era, when it became the residence of Prince Alfred, Duke of Edinburgh. Alfred was Queen Victoria's second son, from 1874 until 1893. During these years Eastwell Manor became something of a country retreat for several of the royals, including the future King Edward VII and Queen Victoria herself, who was actually photographed skating on the lake in winter.

Two of Prince Alfred's daughters were born at Eastwell, Princess Mary, who later became Queen of Romania, and Princess Beatrice, who married the Spanish Prince Alfonso de Orleans y Borbon.

Prince Alfred lived at the manor until 1893, when he inherited the Duchy of Saxe-Coburg and Gotha in Germany and left England for good.

During the 1920s the house was ravaged by fire and had to be largely rebuilt.

Sir John de Fonblanque Pennefather, [29 March 1856 – 8 August 1933] was a British cotton merchant, born in Perth, Australia. Having made his fortune he returned to the UK and was a conservative member of parliament. He became the First Baronet of Golden, a small village in County Tipperary, Ireland. Then, in 1928 he bought Eastwell Manor and demolished much of the old mansion and had it rebuilt to a very high standard, with commendable attention to historic details. Thanks to his good judgement, the manor house, as we see it today, appears true to its Tudor origins of five hundred years ago.

Bruce W. Johnson

Eynsford Castle

A major structure in Eynsford, near Swanley. English Heritage
Postcode for Satnav: DA4 0AA
Nearest major road M20 / A225
Website: https://www.english-heritage.org.uk/visit/places/eynsford-castle/
Parking Arrangements: On street parking.
Public transport: Eynesford Railway Station

Also nearby:
Eynsford village - medieval buildings and medieval bridge
Eagle Heights bird sanctuary
Eynsford to Farningham village walk:
Lullingstone Castle and World Garden
Lullingstone Roman Villa [English Heritage]
Brands Hatch motor racing track.

Description and Defences

The castle stands on a slight man-made mound and would have had a moat around it, with entrance through a stone gatehouse over a drawbridge. There was an outer bailey to the south east but little remains of that.

The most unusual feature of Eynsford Castle is that it doesn't have a keep. Normally a Norman Castle would have a bailey yard with a keep in the middle or at one end, but at Eynsford there is simply the main enclosure and the lord's hall sits within that along with all the other service buildings, which were made of timber and have now disappeared. The hall had at least two storeys, plus cellars. This type of castle, with a simple enclosure and no keep, is technically described as an "enclosure castle" which makes good sense.

The outer wall is nine meters high but for the most part made out of small stones bonded with mortar. This is common in Kent which did not have such good supplies of high quality building stone as may be found in other parts of the country. There is evidence of at least three garde-robes which would have discharged straight into the moat. The remains of the kitchen are still visible, and there was a well. We can only but wonder at the consequences of having a moat full of sewage directly above the area which fed the well.

History

It is believed that there had previously been a wooden Saxon hall on the site, possibly owned by the church, as it was owned by Lanfranc, the first Norman Arch-Bishop of Canterbury, who granted it to Ralph, one of his knights, as was normal under the feudal system. The knight took the name of the castle to become the name of his family, and hence the future owners in each generation were each known as Sir William of Eynsford.

The existing castle was built around 1090 by Ralph's son William de Eynsford I.

His son, William de Eynsford II increased the height of the walls in 1130 at a time when England was suffering from a civil war between King Stephen and the Empress Matilda. He also built a new hall where he and his family would have lived.

Eynsford Castle

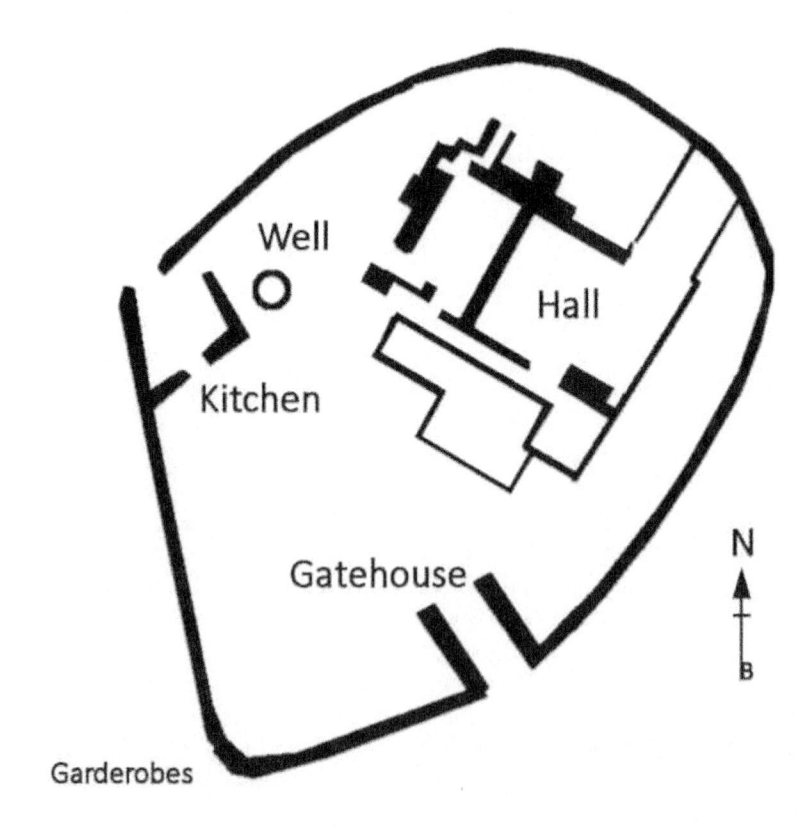

The next William de Eynsford became involved, in a small way, in the events leading up to the death of Thomas Becket. As Lord of the Manor he held the right to appoint the local priest, but the monks of Christ Church, Canterbury also claimed that right. Sir William refused to let their chosen priest enter the church, so Thomas Becket excommunicated him. The King, who was good friend of Sir William, ordered Becket to undo the excommunication, but the argument added to the bad blood which was building up between the king and the clergyman. Eventually this ill-feeling led to the murder of Archbishop Becket. [See also the section on Saltwood Castle.] The killing made Becket a martyr and the Pope made him a saint, which in turn brought a great deal of wealth to Canterbury Cathedral.

Two generations later, William Eynsford V had fought for King John, but turned against him and actually fought in the siege of Rochester Castle. He was captured, narrowly escaped execution and was held prisoner until John died.

The internal buildings were reconstructed around 1250 after a fire.

When the last of the male Eynsfords died out in 1261 the property was divided between William Heringaud and Nicholas de Criol, each of whom was married to a sister of William de Eynsford. Both William and Nicholas sided with Simon de Montfort and the rebel barons fighting against the king. As a result they had their castle confiscated. When the land was returned to them the two brothers in law should really have split it between them, but instead they continued as co-owners, with the Heringaud share being sold down the line to a whole succession of new owners. Meanwhile Ralph de Farningham, who had handled the confiscation, continued to claim that he owned it.

As the years passed there was a long and bitter dispute over the ownership of the castle, leading to a situation where, in 1312, Nicholas de Criol and his men, broke into the building, breaking down the doors and damaging the windows. That raid seems to have marked the end of the castle being used as a residence, although it did come back into the ownership of a single family when the last of the de Criols was beheaded in 1461.

Over the following centuries the castle was used for stabling of animals and even as kennels for hunting dogs, during which time it gradually fell into disrepair. In the Victorian period some local antiquarians paid Edward Cresy to clear the site and carry out a survey. The castle was taken over by the state in 1948 and is now under the care of English Heritage.

Fairseat Castle

A minor structure near West Malling
Postcode for Satnav: ME19 5EG
Nearest major road   M20
Parking Arrangements: Roadside parking

Also nearby
The Coldrum Stones, Neolithic long barrow

Follow Coldrum Lane east from the Coldrum Stones for about 400 yards. Fairseat castle is off the road to the left.

Description and Defences
There is very little to see, just a slight mound in a rectangular enclosure. I would not recommend making a journey just to visit the site but it may be interesting to take a look if you are just cycling by.

Bruce W. Johnson

Folkestone Castle

A major structure in Folkestone
Postcode for Satnav: CT19 5LP
Nearest major road   M20 / A20 A260

Also nearby
Folkestone White Horse
Sugarloaf Hill
Battle of Britain Memorial.
Kent Battle of Britain Museum Trust
Elham Valley Line Trust [Railway Museum]

An excellent place for a healthy walk with the dog or a family picnic on a sunny day. Locally this site is known as Caesar's Camp although there is no evidence at all that there was ever any Roman presence here.

Description and Defences
The massive earthworks are actually the remains of an Iron Age hill fort, and were then re-used by the Normans as the basis of a motte and bailey castle which has long since disappeared.

Fort Amherst

A major structure in Chatham. Operated by Fort Amherst Heritage Trust
Postcode for Satnav: ME4 4UB
Nearest major road   A2
Website: https://www.fortamherst.com/

Parking Arrangements: Beware! Cameras leading to parking fines!

Public transport: Chatham Railway Station

Also nearby
Chatham Historical Dockyard
Rochester Castle
Rochester Cathedral

History
Chatham's harbour areas rose to great importance in the Tudor period when King Henry VIII founded the naval dockyard. Ships from Chatham played a role in the defeat of the Spanish Armada. In 1637 the Dutch were successful in raiding the Medway and capturing the English flagship, the Royal Charles. Slowly, over the next century, a defensive position was constructed on the high ground overlooking the town. Tensions then developed with France, in the American War of Independence and then the Napoleonic Wars, each leading to further improvements in the fortifications.

Description and Defences
The defences at Fort Amherst were ahead of their time, instead of building barracks above ground, large amounts of tunnelling made it possible for troops to be lodged underground where they would be impervious to bombardments from ships' guns.

As was the case at Dover, some of the first ever anti-aircraft guns were deployed at Fort Amherst during the First World War. In fact, the fortifications were of immense importance in both World Wars as they served to protect the Naval Dockyard.

There is a marvellous view from the top of the redoubt, out across the Medway, and it is easy to see what an excellent field of fire this provided for the gun batteries.

There are some very well preserved military tunnels beneath Fort Amherst, including one section which has been restored to its World War Two condition.

Bruce W. Johnson

Garlinge Castle

Also known as Dent de Lion Gate.
A minor structure near Margate. Privately owned
Postcode for Satnav: CT9 5LL
Nearest major road   A28
Parking Arrangements: Roadside

Modern houses have been fitted around the medieval structure so that it is possible to drive straight past without even noticing it. First go to CT9 5LN, then turn into Dent De Lion Road. The first major left turn is into Dent De Lion Court, and there is a car park on the right serving CT9 5LL.

History
Around 1440 John Dent de Lion added fortifications to his manor house in order to guard against raids by the Flemish. It is said that he also used it for smuggling.

The gatehouse has gun loops and once had a portcullis, but the actual height of the wall suggests it was always more decorative than functional.

Garlinge Castle: Dent de Lion Gate

In fact, the property had an uneventful history and did not feature in any sieges of battles that we know of. In 1703 it was rebuilt as a country house. At that time two interesting discoveries were made. One was a Roman burial crypt complete with funerary urns. The other was a medieval bottle dungeon, similar to the one in Saint Andrews Castle in Scotland.

Although nothing else remains, the gatehouse is impressive. For many years it served as a rather grandiose gateway for the local farm.

Around the year 1800 the estate was owned, for a while, by the radical politician Charles James Fox. Even by that time little remained apart from the gatehouse, as evidenced by an engraving by Amelia Nowell from 1797. [Not shown here] In the 19th century the manor house was pulled down and turned into a farm.

During the twentieth century the situation was almost comical, with a housing estate on one side and the farm on the other, with this rather grandiose gate marking the boundary between them. Now it sits entirely surrounded by houses, creating a front street like no other.

Bruce W. Johnson

Gundulph's Tower, Rochester

A major structure in Rochester. English Heritage
Postcode for Satnav: ME1 1QE
Nearest major road   A2
Website: https://www.english-heritage.org.uk/visit/places/rochester-castle/
Parking Arrangements: Short term parking on the Esplanade, directly outside the Castle.
Rochester Riverside Parking ME1 1PZ
Rochester Railway car park ME1 1NH
Blue Boar Car Park ME1 1PD
Public transport: Rochester Railway Station, 2 minute walk.

Also Nearby
Rochester Castle

Description
On the north side of Rochester Cathedral a square, stone tower stands, three stories high between the cross aisles of the Cathedral. The walls are six feet thick and built of coursed ragstone rubble supported with broad but shallow buttresses. Two massive projecting buttresses appear to have been added in the 13th century. Internally the tower is 24ft square.

There has been considerable debate about the origins and use of this structure, with some "experts" claiming it was a bell tower for the church which stood nearby, before the present cathedral was built. Others have suggested it was a repository for records. Both are wrong. Gundulph's Tower is certainly a defensive structure, dating from around 1100 A.D. The evidence for this is that it originally had no windows and a fortified entrance.

There are windows in the walls and two entrances at ground floor level, but all of these are later additions. The original entrance to the building still exists, a vaulted passage at first floor level, which would have been reached by an external stairway. This is a classic defensive feature, designed to make it impossible for attackers to bring up a battering ram to the doors.

The tower is very similar to St. Leonards Tower, at West Malling, and to two other structures found in Oxford, St. Michael's Tower and St. Georges Tower. The medieval church was wealthy at a time when the people suffered grinding poverty and starvation. The most likely purpose of all four structures was to provide a place of safety where monks and priests could take shelter and protect their treasures if rioting mobs attacked their church or monastery.

Hadlow Castle

A major structure near Tonbridge
Postcode for Satnav: TN11 0ED
Nearest major road: A26
Website: http://www.thehadlowtower.co.uk/
Parking Arrangements: On roadside.
Public transport: Train to Tonbridge, Number 7 bus from Quarry Hill Parade, or High Street, heading north towards Maidstone. Disembark at the Maltings, or Hadlow Square. The tower can be seen on the far side of the road.

Also nearby
Tonbridge Castle

Hadlow Castle and Tower c1890

History

In 1790 a local man changed his name from Barton to Walter May as the condition of inheriting a fortune from his uncle's will. Flush with his new wealth he built a Mock Gothic mansion which became known as Hadlow Castle. His son, Walter Barton May, added the tower known as "May's Folly", in 1838. This type of construction was typical of the period. The Romantic Movement was a highly significant phase in British culture, marking a fascination with the beauty of the historical past. Artists painted Pre-Raphaelite fantasies, authors wrote novels embracing both the Age of Chivalry and Gothic horror. Rich gentlemen built grand castles. Even the government joined in with enthusiasm; both Tower Bridge and the Houses of Parliament provide excellent examples of the Mock-Gothic style. With that in mind, we should accept that whilst Hadlow might not be a genuine castle, it is certainly a genuine example of a very important architectural style.

Most of the castle buildings were demolished in 1951, leaving the tower as stands today, somewhat isolated but well known as a prominent local landmark.

Sadly, the tower itself was badly damaged by the great storm of 1987 but was later repaired using funds from the National Lottery and other sources. It is now minus the topmost section, known as the lantern, which was removed for safety reasons as part of the repair work.

Hadlow is now privately owned and has been converted into holiday lets, but it is open on certain Thursdays from May to October. [See website]

Hever Castle

A major site near Sevenoaks, privately owned but open to the public.
Postcode for Satnav: TN8 7NG
Nearest major road   A21
Website: https://www.hevercastle.co.uk/
Parking Arrangements: on site.
Public transport: Hever Railway Station [20 minutes' walk to castle]

Also nearby
Chiddingstone Village and Castle
Edenbridge Village
Penshurst Place
The Forest of the Weald [Area of natural beauty]

Hever Castle: Detail from watercolour by Henry Bright 1859

    Kent is richly blessed with castles. Dover is magnificent and Leeds is beautiful, but Hever is my personal favourite. I first visited the castle around 1980 as a young history teacher leading a school party. I was instantly charmed by its beauty and have never grown tired of it.
    The castle stands within its own sparkling moat, which nowadays plays home to a goodly number of hungry ducks and fishes. The rooms and chambers within are rich in history and with all the beauty of a fairytale palace. Beyond the walls, the Italian Gardens with their marble columns and classical

archways stretch out towards a majestic lake, a scene of pure romance which can seem like paradise rediscovered on a sunny day.

History

It had long been assumed that Hever Castle was built in 1270 AD., by a William de Hever, who was a sheriff in the reign of Edward I. However, in 2022 new research by Architectural Historian, Simon Thurley established that the castle was built more than a hundred years later, around 1383, for Sir John de Cobham.

It thus appears that the most fundamental features of the castle are original structures, perfectly representing both the defensive technology and the domestic living arrangements of the late 14th century. One example which arises from the research was that even within such a compact building, domestic life was strictly divided, with the Lord and his family living in the west wing and the servants living in the east wing, on the other side of the courtyard. Original timbers more than 600 years old have been discovered on the first floor of the west wing, where Anne Boleyn would have lived with her parents at a time when she was being courted by King Henry VIII.

The entrance to the castle is through a gatehouse which includes a drawbridge over the moat, crenelated battlements and machicolations from which missiles could be hurled down upon enemy troops below. There is also a portcullis, one of only three in the country which are thought to still be in working order.

Another fascinating feature is the presence of "gun loops." Up to this point castles tended to have arrow slits, which were long and tall, so that archers could adjust their range by raising their bow higher. Hand guns fired straight ahead, whatever the range of the target, so they did not need slits, but rather circular loops, like small port-holes.

The very first references to firearms, in Britain, date from a naval victory, the Battle of Sluys in 1340, and gunpowder was being manufactured at the Tower of London in 1346. However, these early guns were seen as being much less effective than longbows and generally used more for their effect on enemy morale. It isn't until 1386 that any handguns are listed in the royal treasury.

Viewed in this light, Sir John de Cobham's castle at Hever incorporated technology which was absolutely up to date. This was not just a comfortable manor house, but a solid castle ready for serious conflict.

This, in turn, begs a question. Hever is far from any enemy territory and had no need to fear raids by the French, the Scots or the Welsh. The fact that its owner was investing his fortune in such high quality defences may tell us a great deal about the internal conflicts which troubled England in the Middle-Ages.

The Peasant's Revolt had taken place just two years before the castle received its licence to crennelate. The century which followed was to be marked by civil war. Historians refer to this as the age of the "Over-Mighty Subject," when the great lords of the realm were so rich and so powerful that they could challenge the rule of the king.

Hever Castle

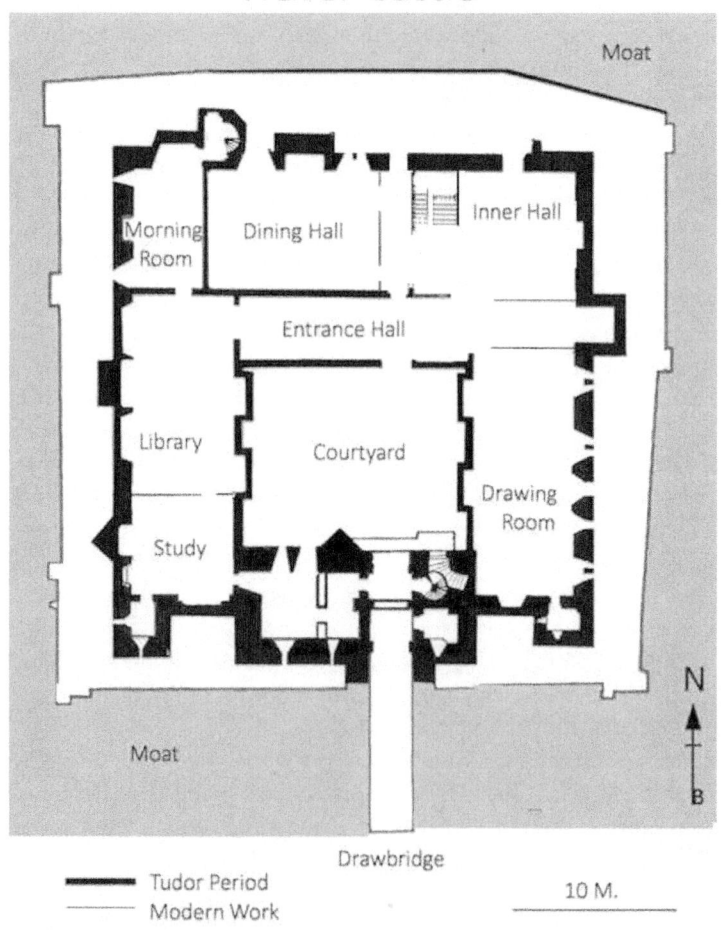

The Earl of Warwick was a perfect example of this phenomenon. During the Wars of the Roses he was considered to have so much power that whichever side he was supporting would come out on top. Thus he is remembered as "Warwick the Kingmaker."

This political instability continued right up to 1485 when Richard III was slain at the Battle of Bosworth Field. This brought an end to the wars of the Roses, and Henry Tudor was crowned as King Henry VII.

Thus, we should understand, Hever Castle was not designed to resist a foreign enemy, but to provide a safe haven from civil strife, and that these internal disturbances were to last until the end of the medieval period, another hundred years into the future.

The castle was sold when Sir John Cobham died, and later sold again in 1423 to Sir Roger Fiennes. In 1462 it was sold once more, this time to Sir Geoffrey Bullen, or Boleyn, a gentleman of property from Norfolk who had risen to become Lord Mayor of London, which suggests that he was financially successful and politically astute. He was also a committed protestant and that would have far reaching implications for the nation in general and his family in particular.

The Boleyns

By 1520 the castle was owned by Sir Thomas Bullen who was a good friend of King, Henry the VIII, serving as Sheriff of Kent and Royal Ambassador. At this time Henry was married to Queen Catherine of Aragon, but the marriage was troubled. Catherine had failed to provide Henry with the son and heir he so desperately wanted. As his love for her waned, he became ever more prone to seeking the favours of others, including Bullen's older daughter. Mary Bullen had grown up at Hever and had become a lady in waiting to Princess Mary, the sister of Henry VIII who was married to the French King.

As a Lady in Waiting to the French Queen, Mary Boleyn spent a number of years in Paris where she gained a reputation for her romantic exploits until in 1519, at the age of 20, she had an affair with King Francis himself. Mary returned to England and was married to a courtier, William Carey, the following year. That very same year she became the mistress of King Henry VIII. It is rumoured that both of her children were fathered by Henry though he never acknowledged them.

William Carey died in 1528, leaving Mary Buleyn a widow at the age of twenty nine. By then, however, Henry's attentions had already shifted to her younger sister Anne. Henry was desperate to settle the succession by having a legitimate male heir, something which his wife, Catherine of Aragon, was never able to provide.

Anne Boleyn was a vibrant young woman, who had been educated in the Netherlands and had then served as a maid of honour to the Austrian Empress, and to two French Queens, Mary and Claude. Anne was intelligent. She was accomplished in mathematics, languages and history as well as music, poetry and dancing. She also undertook a range of sports including archery, horse-riding and hunting.

All of this would have marked Anne out as someone who was likely to make a good marriage. She had been secretly betrothed to Henry Percy, the son of the Earl of Northumberland, but his father had forbidden the match and in 1523 Anne was sent home to Hever and the quiet life. In reality, though, it may not have been all that quiet, because many years later, in 1536, it was revealed that she had been the lover of Sir Thomas Wyatt.

By 1526 Henry began to court Anne, but she was determined to be more than just his mistress and did not give in to him as her sister had done. The fact that Anne had already had dalliances with both Henry Percy and Sir Thomas Wyatt suggests that her reluctance to grapple with the King was based on a genuine desire to become queen, rather than shyness or moral scruples.

By 1527 Anne had withdrawn from the court, in London, and was living in the family home at Hever Castle. This gave her some protection from the King's advances. Kept at long range, he was forced to court her with gentle persuasion.

Of course, Henry could not offer to marry Anne as he was already married to Catherine of Aragon, and despite all his effort the Pope would not grant him a divorce. Such was the importance of the matter that the Pope's ambassador to England made an effort to obtain written evidence, including love letters which Henry wrote to Anne while she was still living at Hever. Henry was claiming that his marriage had never been valid and should therefore be set aside. The Catholic Church would argue that the love letters present matters in a different light, showing that Henry has a long standing and adulterous affair with Anne Boleyn.

Fortunately for historians, these letters were then preserved in the Vatican library and have been published in recent years. In the extracts which follow we can see how their relationship changed and developed over the two years that Anne lived at Hever.

In the first extract, written around May 1527, Anne was still in her early twenties. Henry was 36 and increasingly worried about his succession. At this point he had been focussed on her for around a year already and was still trying to persuade her to become his mistress;

It is absolutely necessary for me to obtain this answer, having been for above a whole year stricken with the dart of love, and not yet sure whether I shall fail of finding a place in your heart and affection, which last point has prevented me for some time past from calling you my mistress because, if you only love me with an ordinary love, that name is not suitable for you, because it denotes a singular love, which is far from common.

But if you please to do the office of a true loyal mistress and friend, and to give up yourself body and heart to me, who will be, and have been, your most loyal servant, (if your rigour does not forbid me) I promise you that not only the name shall be given you, but also that I will take you for my only mistress, casting off all others besides you out of my thoughts and affections, and serve you only.

It seems that Anne replied saying that she was his servant, but not his Mistress, for Henry's next letter says;

Though it is not fitting for a gentleman to take his lady in the place of a servant, yet, complying with your desire, I willingly grant it you, if thereby you can find yourself less uncomfortable in the place chosen by yourself, than you have been in that which I gave you, thanking you cordially that you are pleased still to have some remembrance of me.

King Henry VIII arriving at Hever, by Nash.

Henry continued to court Anne, telling her that he was in fact her servant, and sending her a buck deer which he had killed in his hunting. This might seem rather inappropriate as a love token to modern minds, but venison was a luxury meat at the time, enjoyed only by those who were rich enough to own tracts of forest.

And to cause you yet oftener to remember me, I send you, by the bearer of this, a buck killed late last night by my own hand, hoping that when you eat of it you

may think of the hunter; and thus, for want of room, I must end my letter, written by the hand of your servant, who very often wishes for you instead of your brother.
H. R.

By the time he writes the fourth letter Henry seems to be becoming increasingly desperate, comparing his passions to the heat of the sun.

My Mistress & Friend
My heart and I surrender ourselves into your hands, beseeching you to hold us commended to your favour, and that by absence your affection to us may not be lessened, for it were a great pity to increase our pain, of which absence produces enough and more than I could ever have thought could be felt, reminding us of a point in astronomy which is this: the longer the days are, the more distant is the sun, and nevertheless the hotter; so is it with our love, for by absence we are kept a distance from one another, and yet it retains its fervour, at least on my side; I hope the like on yours, assuring you that on my part the pain of absence is already too great for me; and when I think of the increase of that which I am forced to suffer, it would be almost intolerable, but for the firm hope I have of your unchangeable affection for me: and to remind you of this sometimes, and seeing that I cannot be personally present with you, I now send you the nearest thing I can to that, namely, my picture set in a bracelet, with the whole of the device, which you already know, wishing myself in their place, if it should please you. This is from the hand of your loyal servant and friend.

The next surviving letter, dated July 1527 is, if anything even more beholden to the Lady, with whom he is now exchanging gifts.

For a present so beautiful that nothing could be more so (considering the whole of it), I thank you most cordially, not only on account of the fine diamond and the ship in which the solitary damsel is tossed about, but chiefly for the fine interpretation and the too humble submission which your goodness hath used towards me in this case; for I think it would be very difficult for me to find an occasion to deserve it, if I were not assisted by your great humanity and favour, which I have always sought to seek, and will seek to preserve by all the kindness in my power, in which my hope has placed its unchangeable intention, which says, Aut illic, aut nullibi. (Latin: Either there or nowhere)

Another letter follows a few days later, and we notice that Henry has given his messenger an oral message to pass to Anne, clearly there are some things he would prefer not to write down.

To My Mistress
Consider well, my mistress, that absence from you grieves me sorely, hoping that it is not your will that it should be so; but if I knew for certain that you voluntarily desired it, I could do no other than mourn my ill-fortune, and by degrees abate my great folly.

And so, for lack of time, I make an end of this rude letter, beseeching you to give credence to this bearer in all that he will tell you from me.

Written by the hand of your entire Servant,
H.R.

King Henry VIII and Anne Boleyn in the gallery, by Nash.

Another letter to Anne was written the following year, in February 1528. He states that "You and I shall have our desired end." This may indicate that he had proposed to marry Anne, and she had accepted, though, of course, this could only happen if his marriage to Catherine of Aragon was annulled.

Darling,
These shall be only to advertise you that this bearer and his fellow be despatched with as many things to compass our matter, and to bring it to pass as our wits could imagine or devise; which brought to pass, as I trust, by their diligence, it shall be shortly, you and I shall have our desired end, which should be more to my heart's ease, and more quietness to my mind, than any other thing in the world.

During that year there is a radical change in the tone of the letters. Henry is writing to her three times a month, but alongside his professions of love there are all sorts of pieces of everyday business and news.

In the summer of 1528 the country was swept by a pandemic of plague or flue referred to at the time as the sweating sickness. The letters show that Anne took ill while Henry was away so he sent her one of his royal physicians.

When she asked him to help her sister, who had fallen pregnant,. Henry agreed that the father, Walter Weltze, should be expected stand by her.

The following month he reports that more of his courtiers have taken ill, but that is not his only concern. It seems that Anne has got involved in some intrigues regarding a convent. A new abbess is about to be chosen and Anne feels that the nuns who are already there are immoral and unsuitable. She has pressured the king to have the place investigated and to make sure that someone more suitable is chosen.

In late July he writes how much he is looking forward to being with her again, his tone very much suggesting that they now have a romantic relationship;

The approach of the time for which I have so long waited rejoices me so much, that it seems almost to have come already. However, the entire accomplishment cannot be till the two persons meet, which meeting is more desired by me than anything in this world; for what joy can be greater upon earth than to have the company of her who is dearest to me, knowing likewise that she does the same on her part, the thought of which gives me the greatest pleasure.

In August he goes further, writing a letter which clearly indicates that their relationship is now of a sexual nature, as reflected in the final sentence;

Mine own sweetheart, this shall be to advertise you of the great elengeness that I find here since your departing ; for, I ensure you methinketh the time longer since your departing now last, than I was wont to do a whole fortnight. I think your kindness and my fervency of love causeth it ; for, otherwise, I would not have thought it possible that for so little a while it should have grieved me. But now that I am coming towards you, methinketh my pains be half removed; and also I am right well comforted in so much that my book maketh substantially for my matter; in looking whereof I have spent above four hours this day, which causeth me now to write the shorter letter to you at this time, because of some pain in my head; wishing myself (especially an evening) in my sweetheart's arms, whose pretty dukkys I trust shortly to kiss.

A few days later he tells her that he has been arranging lodgings for her;

Darling,

Though I have scant leisure, yet, remembering my promise, I thought it convenient to certify you briefly in what case our affairs stand.

As touching a lodging for you, we have got one by my lord cardinal's means, the like whereof could not have been found hereabouts for all causes, as this bearer shall more show you.

As touching our other affairs, I assure you there can be no more done, nor more diligence used, nor all manner of dangers better both foreseen and provided for, so that I trust it shall be hereafter to both our comforts, the specialities whereof were both too long to be written, and hardly by messenger to be declared. Wherefore, till you repair hither, I keep something in store, trusting it shall not be long to; for I have caused my lord, your father, to make his provisions with speed; and thus for lack of time, darling, I make an end of my letter, written with the hand of him which I would were yours.

In September 1528 he wrote to tell her that the Papal legate had arrived, in effect, Henry was putting forward his case for the divorce of his wife.

The reasonable request of your last letter, with the pleasure also that I take to know them true, causeth me to send you these news. The legate which we most desire arrived at Paris on Sunday or Monday last past, so that I trust by the next Monday to hear of his arrival at Calais, and then I trust within a while after to enjoy that which I have so long longed for, to God's pleasure and our both comforts.

No more to you at this present, mine own darling, for lack of time, but that I would you were in mine arms, or I in yours, for I think it long since I kissed you.

In fact, despite all of Henry's high hopes the Pope would never grant him a divorce, because Henry's existing wife was the sister of the King of Spain, who effectively had control of the Pope. The negotiations dragged on until 1532. Things then took on another course. Such was the king's determination, or perhaps his desperation, that eventually he decided to break away from the Roman Catholic Church, thus launching the Protestant Reformation in England.

Henry and Anne married secretly in November 1532 and had an official wedding on 25th January 1533. On 23rd May the King had his former marriage nullified. Anne was crowned Queen of England on June 1st and gave birth to her daughter, Elizabeth, on the 7th of September.

Anne failed to provide Henry with a son and her fall from grace was catastrophic. In 1536 she was executed by decapitation after being found guilty of adultery and incest. Normally, when powerful nobles were executed in Tudor times, their lands were confiscated by the crown. In the case of Anne Boleyn, her parents were not charged with any crime and were allowed to live out the remainder of their lives at Hever. This strongly suggests that Henry knew she was not really guilty of any crime.

Anne of Cleves

Meanwhile, King Henry VIII continued to long for a male heir. His third wife, Jane Seymour, died in 1537 and he then married a German Princess, Anne of Cleves, who arrived in England at Deal Castle on the 27th of December 1539.

It is often suggested that Henry's choice of bride had been influenced by a painting, composed by Hans Holbien the younger, which made her look slimmer and more attractive than she really was. Whether this is true or not, the marriage was unsuccessful from the start. At one point on her journey to London, Anne was surrounded by a group of masked men. One of them tried to kiss her but she pushed him away, not realising that the masked man was Henry and this was meant to be a romantic prank. Disappointed with his bride to be, Henry said "I like her not" and "I see nothing in this woman as men report of her."

He tried to have the marriage contract cancelled but in the end they went through with the wedding. Things then went from bad to worse as a result of Henry's failings in the marriage bed. Anne was 24 years old and innocent in the ways of men. Henry was 48, overweight and unable to rise to the occasion. Of course Henry blamed Anne, saying to Thomas Cromwell

"I liked her before not well, but now I like her much worse"

After four nights he gave up and within six months the couple were divorced.

For Thomas Cromwell, the failure of the marriage was the cause of his downfall. He had arranged it and as a result he was charged with treason!

Anne seems to have handled the situation well. She agreed to the divorce without a fuss, and this avoided a diplomatic row between England and Cleeves. Henry was grateful and rewarded her for her co-operation. On the day that their marriage was annulled he wrote;

"You shall find us a perfect friend, content to repute you as our dearest sister. We shall, within five or six days...determine your state, minding to endow you with £4000 of yearly revenue ... your loving brother and friend, Henry."

The king was good to his word. Anne of Cleves did not lose her head, as Anne Boleyn had done. Instead she remained on friendly terms with the king. She was even invited to Hampton Court for Christmas, where she played cards with Henry and danced with his new queen, Catherine Howard. In addition to her yearly income she was given a number of properties;

Richmond Palace, Bletchingly Palace, Anne of Cleves House in Lewes, lands in Hampshire taken from Braemore Priory and Southwick Priory, and the lease of Hever for the rest of her life, and so the castle entered a new phase as the luxurious manor house of an independent lady. Recent research carried out by Simon Thurley, on behalf of the castle's owners, has established that Anne of Cleves arranged for a considerable amount of building work to be undertaken, principally, the staircase gallery and the splendid long gallery.

Long galleries were extremely popular in the Tudor period. In good weather it was fashionable to entertain guests by walking round the castle gardens, but when it rained the Tudor aristocrats would get their exercise by taking guests for a tour of the gallery, which would be decorated with portraits of family members.

When Henry died, in 1547, Anne of Cleves continued to reside at Hever. She also converted to Catholicism, so as to live in peace with the new queen Mary Tudor. Anne died in 1557, the longest surviving out of all of Henry's wives.

The following year, in 1558, the castle was sold to the Waldegrave family.

The Waldorf Astor Era

For the next four hundred years the building was allowed to decline, and was almost a ruin by the start of the twentieth century. Then, in 1903, the castle was bought by an American millionaire, Mr. William Waldorf Astor, who wished to use it as his private home. He became a British subject and in 1917 he was created Viscount Astor of Hever Castle.

Many aspects of the castle, as we see it today, are a tribute to the work of Mr Astor. From the high quality woodwork to the landscaped gardens, it all bears his imprint.

Organisations such as English Heritage and the National Trust do an excellent job in protecting and administering a wide range of sites and buildings. Often they have stepped in when private individuals have simply been unable to afford the upkeep of extensive properties. We owe them a great deal of respect for the work they do. Nevertheless, I suspect that anyone visiting Hever can appreciate that Mr Astor also provided a great service to the country by virtue of the immense investment he made in restoring Hever Castle and constructing its gardens.

The works undertaken are too numerous to fully report, but they included extensive refurbishing and preservation of the ancient woodwork. The final effect is sumptuous.

The old farm buildings standing around the castle were demolished. A network of landscaped gardens were created, making good use of natural rocky outcrops. A vast geometrical garden, known as the Italian Garden runs down to a scenic lake which was created by diverting the local River Eden.

Hever Castle: The Long Gallery

There was, of course, one great danger in all of this. Mr Astor wished to live in the castle and to entertain friends there. This could have led to modernisation which would have obliterated many of the original features. Fortunately he had the presence of mind to chart a different course. A single-storeyed luxury house was built behind the castle, surrounded by smaller buildings to house both guests and servants, the whole project expertly disguised to look like a Tudor village.

In recent memory the castle has suffered from disastrous flooding but has been restored. It remains in private hands but is open to the public.

In my own opinion, the most admirable aspect of the castle is not a defensive feature at all. Most of the castles which we see up and down the country still have their outer wall but have lost the buildings which were once all tucked inside of it. At Hever we see the castle as it ought to be, with its ancient buildings packed in to leave just a small courtyard at the centre. The effect is almost magical and has to be seen, looking out through the upstairs windows and into that timeless area.

Whilst there are many excellent castles in Kent, Hever stands out as my personal favourite as a superb destination for a visit. I would even go so far as to say that no photograph can really do justice to Hever, because perfect setting of the castle in its moat and the classical beauty of the gardens can only be fully appreciated when experienced in person. Certainly I would urge you to walk all the way down through the magnificent Italian Gardens to the very end where you can sit comfortably beneath the marble arches and gaze out over the lake.

In addition to the wonderful building and gardens, there is a golf course, and various playgrounds and activities to amuse the children, not least, feeding the voracious ducks and fishes which live in the castle moat.

Living in a castle

One outstanding feature of Hever is that it is actually possible to stay at the castle. Behind the main building there is what appears to be a picturesque historical village, but it was actually constructed as accommodation for the guests who visited Mr Astor when he owned Hever. More than a hundred years have passed and it is really a remarkable experience for ordinary people to be able to enjoy those rooms where Edwardian millionaires once spent their vacations.

I have personally stayed at Hever as a paying guest, most recently in 2022 and I found it to be a truly delightful experience. Each room is different, though all are of a very high standard. There is also a breakfast room, a reading room and even a billiard room, all of them as you would expect of living in a castle, with timbered ceilings, massive fireplaces and antique furnishings.

All of this combines to ensure that staying at Hever is a truly luxurious experience. At the time of writing, in 2022, there were a variety of options including beautiful rooms and a magnificent holiday cottage called Medley Court. I would advise you to book well in advance in advance in order to enjoy the widest range of rooms and prices.

At the time of writing, the castle did not serve evening meals, but there are local pubs which serve food; the King Henry VIII in Hever village and the Wheatsheaf [TN8 7NU] which we particularly enjoyed.

There is also a camp-site in the local area but be aware that it is about twenty minutes' walk from the castle.

Wedding Venue

At the time of writing [2022] Hever was available as a high quality wedding venue. See the castle's own website for full details.

Ightham Mote

A major structure near Sevenoaks. National Trust
Postcode for Satnav: TN15 0NT
Nearest major road A21 / A25
Website: https://www.nationaltrust.org.uk/ightham-mote
Parking Arrangements: Large car park on site
Public transport:

Also nearby
Ightham Village
Oldbury Hill, woodland walk.
Knole House
Old Soar Manor

Ightham Village, Kent.

Some books on castles simply do not include Ightham Mote, because they classify it as being merely a fortified manor house. Whilst I understand their reasoning I cannot follow their example. I first visited Ightham in 1981and have constantly felt drawn back by its beauty. The whole site is so peaceful and secluded that it has all the charm of a fairy-tale, and yet it has come so close to being lost that its survival must be seen as a glittering triumph for the skilled workers who have carried out restoration, and those who have funded them.

The Ightham Mote estate is full of surprises. We expect castles to be at the top of a hill, but here we walk down from the car-park into a secluded valley, where the only background noise is the trickling of water from natural springs.

At the bottom of the valley stands a manor house, constructed from stone with massive timber beams, and surrounded by its own defensive moat and decorative gardens.

History

The local village would have been established in Anglo-Saxon times as Ehta-Ham, meaning "The village of Ehta." By 1336 Ightham had a parish church and permission from King Edward II to hold an annual fair.

Thomas Cawne is recorded as being owner of Ightham Mote around 1360. Thomas was from a family which had prospered through business, but he left home to fight in the Hundred Years War and earned a name for himself as a successful leader. He was entrusted by Edward, the Black Prince, to manage the castle Neuberg in Normandy and was knighted for his service.

Thomas had effectively risen from the urban middle class to become a member of the gentry. When he returned to England during a break in the fighting he purchased Ightham in order to be close to the court in London, and married Lora Moraunt, the daughter of a local gentleman. Their son Robert inherited Ightham Mote, but he had no children, in fact it is believed that he once tried to kill his wife by throwing her down a well!

On his death the estate passed to his sister Alice, who married a very wealthy heir, called Nicholas Haute. Nicholas was younger than Alice and after her death he married Eleanor Tyrell, who was also from a rich family. He was powerful and influential in local society, serving as Sheriff of Kent and Member of Parliament.

When Sir Nicholas Haute died around 1415 his son William inherited the family estates, including Ightham Mote. He continued the family pattern of marrying for money, his second wife being Joan Woodville, whose aunt Elizabeth married King Edward IV, one of the main participants in the "Wars of the Roses." Through this marriage the Haute family effectively moved from the gentry to the aristocracy. In 1462 Ightham passed to Richard Haute who made significant improvements the house in keeping with his immense wealth.

The Wars of the Roses continued and at one point Richard's estates were seized by the crown and transferred to his brother James, but were later returned when Richard was pardoned.

In 1487 the property passed to Edward Haute who was only aged eleven and seems to have been prone to unsound decisions and bad behaviour. He wasted his fortune, ruined his family and lost the property.

In the Tudor period Ightham was owned by Richard Clement. He appears to have served as an administrator under Henry VII and achieved the title of "Gentleman of the Household." He purchased Ightham Mote for £400 in

1521. By this time Henry VIII was on the throne and he knighted Clement in 1529, possibly as a reward for his work as a magistrate. The Tudor kings never forgot the lessons of the Wars of the Roses and they liked local gentlemen who were powerful enough to keep law and order, but not strong enough to challenge the crown.

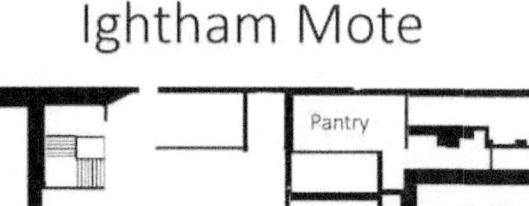

Ightham Mote

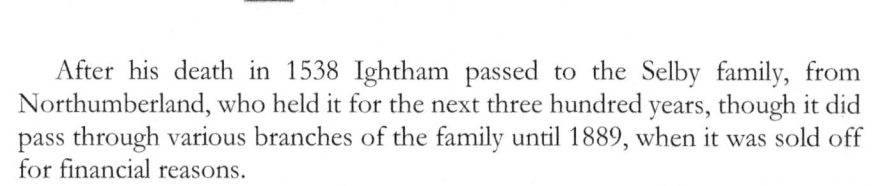

After his death in 1538 Ightham passed to the Selby family, from Northumberland, who held it for the next three hundred years, though it did pass through various branches of the family until 1889, when it was sold off for financial reasons.

The next owner, Thomas Colyer-Fergusson, recognised the need for repair and maintenance and he spent considerable sums on conservation work. Sadly one of his sons died in the Great War and another in the Second Wold War. His grandson, James Colyer Fergusson inherited the property in 1951 but did not have sufficient wealth to manage it properly. He therefore put the lands, the house, and its contents up for sale.

The main house was in real danger of being demolished at this point but three local businessmen realised its importance and purchased it for £5,500. This created a period of breathing space for the building and in August 1952 it was given Grade I listed building status. The rescue was completed in 1953 when Ightham Mote was bought by Charles Henry Robinson. Robinson had visited Ightham in the 1920s and had never forgotten it. By 1953, he had become a successful businessman in the United States and when he saw an advertisement in Country Life Magazine he came to England immediately and made an offer. Then he had second thoughts on his way home and decided to back out of the deal. He wrote a letter while crossing the Atlantic on board the Queen Mary to withdraw from the sale, but the liner's post office was closed, and the letter was never sent. Later on the voyage he changed his mind.

For the next thirty years Mister Robinson lived in Ightham Mote and refurnished it. Many of the items he owned are still in the house as part of the collections. It was during this period that I first visited Ightham, leading a party of schoolchildren from Gillingham. There was something almost magical in stepping away from the urban environment of the Medway Towns to visit a place of such old-world charm hidden away in the very same county.

Charles Henry Robinson bequeathed Ightham Mote to the National Trust and it passed into their care when he died in 1985. This course of action was noble and generous. In time it would also prove to be very fortunate.

After taking possession of the house, the National Trust began a comprehensive programme of restoration, particularly involving woodwork which is vulnerable to both dampness and infestation. The work took twenty years and was completed to the highest standards, winning a number of awards.

Among professional conservators it is often said that all of the work they do ultimately pays for itself. Spending a thousand pounds on conserving a painting tends to add more than that to the lasting value of the painting, so all of the money is spent in a good cause. The National Trust recognised the value of Ightham and the importance of preserving it. Unfortunately they could not have imagined what would follow. In June 2016 Ightham Mote suffered catastrophic flooding, due to heavy rain, with significant damage to all of the ground floor rooms. Having so recently finished the major conservation programme, the National Trust then had to manage a further clean up and repair of the flood damaged areas.

It is difficult to imagine that all the works of the past thirty years could have been completed if the house was still in private hands. If ever there was need of an argument to support the existence of the National Trust, then the story of Ightham Mote would provide an excellent case in point.

Since 2021 there has been a new car-park which is further from the house, but still only a few minutes' walk. This has made it possible to improve the area known as the walled garden. At the time of writing, [2022] there was also a good second-hand bookshop.

Kingsgate Castle

A major structure near Broadstairs. Privately owned
Postcode for Satnav: CT10 3PH
Nearest major road A28 - B2052

Kingsgate Castle

History

Henry Vassal-Fox, later known as Lord Holland, was a leading figure in British politics from 1796 until his death in 1840. As a nephew of Charles James Fox, he became a leading figure among the liberal group known as the Whigs.

Kingsgate Castle was his personal vanity project, a residence by the seaside made to look like a medieval castle. It is therefore an example of what people often call a "Folly." These are buildings which, for decorative purposes, are made to look like historical remains, such as Greek temples.

With this in mind, the structure does have a certain kind of historical value, as it can be seen as an example of the Gothic tastes which prevailed at the time of the Romantic Movement.

The castle is built from normal house bricks, but faced in stone to make it look realistic.

At the start of the twentieth century the castle was restored by a new owned, Lord Lubbock, and over the next forty years it was occupied by people who could reasonably be described as the idle rich, wealthy individuals who enjoyed having a seaside palace while spending their money on drinking and gambling.

After the Second World War, the castle was used as a holiday hotel, but with tragic consequences; John Haigh, better known as the "Acid Bath Murderer" met with a married couple called the Hendersons while they were on holiday. He later lured them back to his place in Croydon where he killed them, drank a glass of their blood, and destroyed their remains in a vat of acid.

The flight of steps which lead down the side of the cliff to the beach, are thought to have been the inspiration for the story of the "Thirty Nine Steps."

In modern times the castle has been divided up into private apartments. It occupies a magnificent position on top of the cliffs, and makes a useful background for holiday photographs.

There is no official website for the castle but some interesting information can be found here:
https://kingsgatecastle.wordpress.com/

Knole House

A major site near Sevenoaks. National Trust
Postcode for Satnav: TN15 0RP
Nearest major road   M25 / A225
Website: https://www.nationaltrust.org.uk/knole
Parking Arrangements: Parking for visitors. All persons in the car must have booked tickets.
Public transport: Train to Sevenoaks, then walk or take 402 Bus to Knole Lane [NOT 402a or 402b]

Also nearby:
Oldbury Hill Iron Age Fort
Sevenoaks Wildlife Reserve

Knole: Detail from a work by Norris

Description
Knole was constructed as a palace for the Archbishops of Canterbury, from 1426 onwards. It therefore comes after the medieval period and can be seen as a prime example of Tudor architecture, typified by its towering redbrick chimney-stacks, with some later remodelling.

History
Henry VIII is said to have hunted in the grounds of the palace and his daughter, Mary Tudor, lived here before succeeding to the throne.

Bruce W. Johnson

Knole: The Gallery, by Nash

In 1603 the palace was obtained by the Sackville family, however they lost much of their wealth during the civil war period and only managed to hang on to the house by selling off much of the furniture and paintings. Subsequently, however, Richard Sackville, 5th Earl of Dorset, married a wealthy wife, Frances Cranfield, and many treasures which had belonged to her father are now housed at Knole.

Charles Sackville, the 6th Earl of Dorset, added even more treasures to the collection, but spent so much that he went bankrupt. Fortunately his son, Lionel Sackville enjoyed a successful career in the government of the new Georgian King George I and became the first Duke of Dorset in 1720, as well as restoring the family fortunes.

His grandson, John Frederick Sackville, 3rd Duke of Dorset, was another great patron of the arts, and a friend of Sir Joshua Reynolds. He expanded the collection at Knole to the point where it now has international significance as a collection of old masters.

One particularly interesting item on show is a statue of a dancer, called 'La Baccelli' who lived with the Duke at Knole and bore him a son. It is said that in 1790 the Duke married a wealthy English heiress called Arabella Cope, and the statue of "La Baccelli" had to be hidden away in the attic.

Knole: The bedchamber by Nash.

Cautionary note

I would respectfully advise readers to be very careful with their spellings when making arrangements, bookings or invitations. Knole is the stately home managed by the National Trust. There is also another location in Kent which is called Knowle Country House. It is a wedding venue between Gravesend and Chatham. It could, perhaps, be embarrassing to turn up at the wrong one.

Bruce W. Johnson

Leeds Castle

A major site near Maidstone. Privately owned but open to the public.
Postcode for Satnav: ME17 1PL
Nearest major road   M20
Website: https://leeds-castle.com/
Parking Arrangements: On site for visitors
Public transport: Train to Bearstead Station [See website for taxi details]

Also nearby
Doddington Place [Gardens] ME9 0BB
Belmont House and Gardens ME13 0HH
Bredgar and Wormshill Railway ME9 8AT

Leeds Castle

   Often described as the most beautiful castle in England, this spectacular structure proves quite fascinating to visitors of all ages and interests. Outwardly it stands as a spectacular example of a medieval fortress, rising proudly from its own shimmering moat, complete with drawbridges, battlements and towers. Historic, romantic and majestic, it has all the charm and promise of a fairytale palace. That, however, is only the first part of

Castles of Kent

what the guest will experience. Within the building further themes are explored, charting the story of the castle and its owners from the conflicts of the Middle-Ages, to the wealthy socialites of the Twentieth Century. Around the estate there are many more attractions and activities, some of them quite unique, and all in all there is every good reason why guests return month after month and year after year to enjoy once again this breataking site.

At the time of writing, [2022] there were several playground adventure areas for children, including a mock castle, an impressive maze and a mysterious grotto. Visitors to the castle could also enjoy falconry displays and even a museum devoted to historic dog-collars!

When entering the main castle area I would strongly advise visitors to make the most of the exhibitions and multi-media presentations which are staged in the rooms of the gatehouse. These are constantly improving and they do help to set the scene for the tour which follows. In particular they will help to explain how the castle has constantly changed and evolved over the centuries.

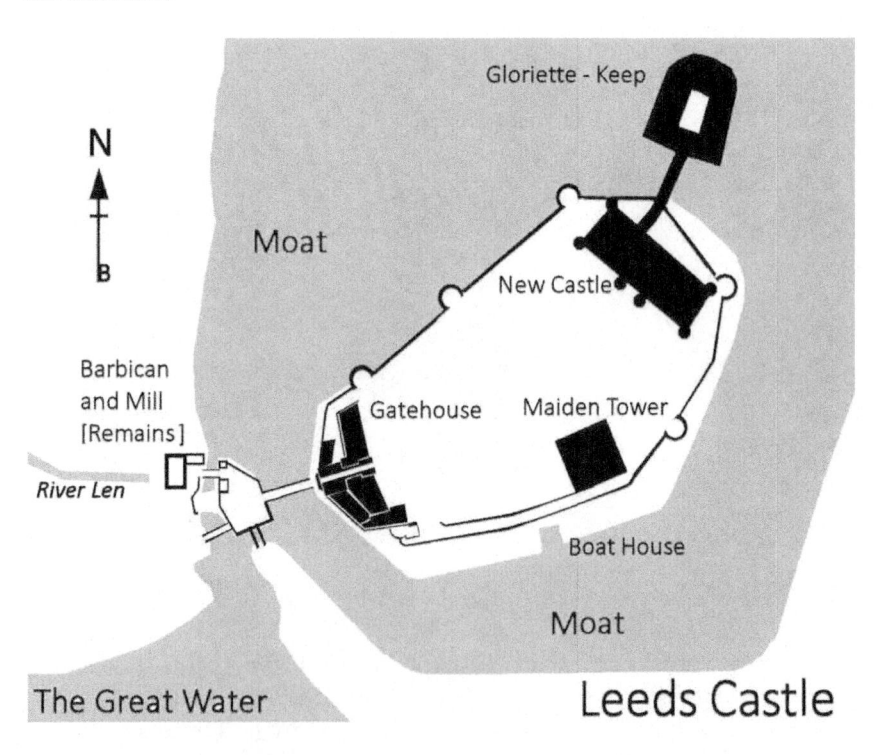

Map of Leeds Castle showing: N (north arrow), Gloriette - Keep, Moat, New Castle, Barbican and Mill [Remains], Gatehouse, Maiden Tower, River Len, Boat House, Moat, The Great Water

Leeds Castle

Description and Defences

The castle is made up of two main sections, each standing on its own small island. The main part of the castle was the bailey, where there would have been buildings such as stables, workshops and barracks. The keep, or Gloriette, stood on the smaller island.

There is actually a third, very small, island, which forms the base for the entrance way, but this is only obvious when seen in a plan or an aerial photograph.

The first line of defence was a very sturdy stone building known as a barbican, a small castle protecting the gates of the main castle. This structure incorporated a flour mill for use in peacetime, but its walls and gates were strong and defensible. Enemy troops would have to capture this before they could even begin to assault the main gatehouse, their task made all the more difficult by the use of several drawbridges.

The next defensive line was the curtain wall, surrounding the bailey yard. At one time there may have been a cross-wall running north-west across the bailey yard, providing another line of defence. The last place of refuge was the keep, although for most of the castle's history this was actually a rather luxurious dwelling place for the aristocrats, and was known as the Gloriette, which means pavilion, reminding us that the castle was not only a military base, but also a luxurious dwelling.

History

Visitors frequently ask why the castle is called Leeds when it is in Kent. As early as 857 A.D. a Kentish noble called Led diverted the river Len to create two small islands, where he built his wooden castle. After the Norman Conquest the site was owned by Bishop Odo and then by Hamon de Crevecoeur, and is referred to in the Domesday survey as "Esleds."

In the modern age we often hear the complaint that history books have understated the role played by women in the affairs of the past. At Leeds, however, we can enjoy learning how a number of famous and powerful women played leading roles over a thousand years of the castle's history. The castle was given as a gift by several kings to their brides, and is often seen as having a particular attraction to ladies. In fact, Leeds Castle is has sometimes been referred to as the "Castle of Queens, Queen of Castles".

Robert de Crevecoeur had the castle rebuilt in stone, around 1119. Then, in the 1130s there was a civil war in England, between King Stephen and the Empress Matilda.

Matilda was the only legitimate heir of King Henry I, but after his death her cousin, Stephen of Blois, claimed the throne, leading to nineteen years of civil war, sometimes referred to as "The Anarchy."

The de Crevour family supported Matilda, and the castle was besieged by King Stephen's forces in 1139, but it was held without capture.

During the reign of Henry III another Robert de Crevecoeur was forced to surrender control of the castle to Sir Roger de Leybourne. His son, William de Leybourne then gave the castle to his friend King Edward I in 1272. Edward took a great liking to the place, which he visited often and he, in turn, gifted it to his queen, Eleanor of Castile.

Eleanor supported her husband during the Second Barons' War, even recruiting archers from France to serve in his army. As far as we can tell the couple were devoted to one another. Edward is one of the very few English Kings who is not known to have had extra-marital affairs.

Eleanor was better educated than most medieval queens and exerted a strong cultural influence on the nation. She was a keen patron of literature and of the decorative arts. When she arrived in England she introduced the Spanish custom of hanging tapestries on walls, a form of decoration which became widespread during her lifetime. She enjoyed having fine tableware, elegantly decorated knives, and even forks - which were something of a new idea, brought back from the east by travellers. She also loved ornamental gardens, especially water features, which were popular in Castille due to the influence of the Islamic Arts. All of these features would have been found in the beautiful "Gloriette" which she established at Leeds Castle, with its picturesque fountain at the centre.

Edward also added to the castle's defences, building an outer wall around the very edge of the main island. With the passing of the years most of the original inner wall has been removed, and Edward's addition is now the main circuit wall which we see today.

After Eleanor's death Edward was grief stricken, but with only one son, he felt he must take steps to ensure the succession. After a five year war against Phillip IV of France, he married Phillip's step-sister, Margaret, as part of the peace treaty! He was 60 and she was just 20, but they had a good marriage. She was respected for her beauty, her piety and her kindness. Edward gave her Leeds Castle as a gift, and so it became something of a tradition that Kings would give it as a love-token to their wives.

This was not always the case, however. One exception to this was that Edward II gifted the castle to a certain Lord Badlesmere. It was destined to play an important part in the man's downfall.

Edward II came to the throne in 1307, the one surviving son of Eleanor of Castile. His reign was troubled. He outraged opinion by having a male favourite, Piers Gaveston, who was kidnapped and executed by a group of barons in 1312. Edward then lost the Battle of Bannockburn to Robert the Bruce in 1314. In the years which followed there was famine and the King found a new male favourite, Hugh Despencer, who outraged the ruling class both by his immorality and his acts of lawlessness, stealing land in Wales and committing piracy against the towns of the south coast.

Taking all of these issues together it should be no surprise that some of the barons began to plot against Edward. He sent his long-time friend, Lord Badlesmere, north, possibly to spy on them, but instead Badlesmere also began to voice a degree of opposition to the King, as detailed in the section on Chilham Castle.

Considering this opposition to be treachery, and hungry for revenge, King Edward arranged for Queen Isabella to go on a pilgrimage to Canterbury and to ask for a night's accommodation at Leeds Castle, on her return journey. This was clearly a deliberate ploy, as it involved a significant detour from the usual route.

Badlesmere's wife fell right into the trap and refused entry to the Queen in October 1321. In response Queen Isabella ordered her soldiers to force an entry. Lady Badlesmere told her archers to open fire and six of the Queen's men were killed. This gave Edward the excuse he wanted to attack the castle with a substantial army of soldiers borrowed from his allies and 500 men from the City of London. Those Earls who supported the King were quick to turn up in support, but those who opposed him held back as they were afraid to come out openly as rebels. Leeds Castle surrendered after five days, on October 31st, and thirteen men of its garrison were executed. Lady Badlesmere and her children were imprisoned in the Tower of London, and later in Dover Castle. Her husband was defeated, captured and executed without mercy.

These severe actions only caused the barons, led by Lancaster, to become even more opposed to Edward, but with support from his new favourite, Hugh Despenser, he managed to put down his challengers. The turning point came when Queen Isabella tuned against him, mainly due to her hatred of Despenser.

Isabella began to have a relationship with an exiled lord, Roger Mortimer, and together with her son, Edward they landed at Orwell in 1326. The country flocked to support them probably due to their loathing of the corrupt government. Bishop Stapledon of Exeter was actually executed by a mob and his head sent Isabella.

In victory, Isabella and Mortimer showed themselves to be ruthless in dealing with their enemies. Hugh Despenser was executed, hacked to pieces, and his body fed to the dogs. His son, Hugh Despenser the younger, was stripped by the mob and had biblical verses scrawled on his skin, he was then sentenced to be hanged, until almost dead, castrated, drawn through the town [ie. dragged behind a horse] then cut into quarters while still alive.

Isabella's husband, King Edward II was first imprisoned then murdered in Berkley Castle in 1327. There have always been disturbing rumours about how his death took place.

For a short while Mortimer and Isabella ruled the country but in 1330 the young Edward III took revenge for his father's murder, by kidnapping and killing Mortimer.

Isabella was allowed to live out her life, but was generally disliked and referred to as "The She-Wolf of France." She returned to Leeds Castle, claiming that it was hers by right of dowry. Her full story is too long to cover here but it is indeed quite remarkable, and well worth reading up on.

The next King, Edward III, had been married to Philipa of Hainault in 1327. Her exact age is unknown but she was under 18, perhaps as young as 12. She was a loyal and hardworking Queen. Edward did not grant her the castle but he made several improvements to the defences and she stayed there with him.

Richard II continued the tradition of treating Leeds as a "Ladies Castle" by gifting it to his wife, Anne of Bohemia in 1382. They were both only fifteen years old when they married, but they lived happily together for 12 years. Richard II was the "boy-king" who had to face up to the Peasants Revolt. It is generally believed that Anne was a good influence on him even helping to get some of the rebels pardoned.

Anne died of the plague, at Sheen Manor in 1394. Edward was so upset that he had the building demolished! We should probably give thanks that she did not die at Leeds Castle instead.

Leeds Castle surrounded by its moat.

In 1403 Henry IV gave the castle to Joanne of Navarre, who was generally unpopular with the public because she preferred the company and advice of her own Breton entourage. In 1413 her husband Henry IV died and in 1415 she fell out with his son, Henry V, which led to her being imprisoned and having her wealth confiscated. Some accounts say that she was charged with witchcraft, but this was really just a means for locking someone up without any actual crime being proven. In any case, after three years, Henry relented and she was released and her fortune was restored.

Henry V was the great soldier king, who won the Battle of Agincourt. He married Catherine of Valois in 1420, as part of the peace treaty he made with France. He continued the tradition by gifting Leeds Castle to his queen. Sadly he died of sickness at the siege of Meaux in 1422, without ever having seen their son, the future King Henry VI.

Catherine's grandson, by her second marriage, was the Welsh nobleman, Henry Tudor, who was effectively the last man standing at the end of the Wars of the Roses. He became King Henry VII of England.

His son, King Henry VIII owned the castle in 1520 at the time of his extravagant meeting with King Francois of France, an event known to history as "The Field of the Cloth of Gold." Up to 12,000 people attended the pageant, which, among other things, is famous for the temporary portable palace which the English took with them. A stunning painting of the whole event still exists in Leeds Castle.

Henry VIII claimed to have transformed Leeds from a castle to a palace, adding the upper storey to the Gloriette and building the Maidens Tower. He subsequently gave the castle to his good friend, Sir Thomas Ledger, thus ending its 300 year status as a royal castle. However that does not mark its last involvement with the Queens of England, as Henry's daughter Elizabeth was kept there as a prisoner by her sister Mary. After Mary's death she was crowned as Queen Elizabeth I.

In the years which followed the castle was passed or sold to several new owners.

Sir Richard Smythe built a Jacobean house in the centre, but it was later pulled down.

Sir Thomas Culpepper, and his family were Parliamentary supporters during the English Civil War. As a result, the castle was not destroyed after Parliament's victory as so many sadly, were. In 1665, however, when the castle was owned by another Sir Thomas Culpepper, it was used as a jail for Dutch prisoners of war, who started a fire and badly damaged the gloriette.

Catherine Culpepper married Thomas, 5th Lord Fairfax of Cameron in 1690. At the time of writing [2022] the stone-flagged "Servants Hall" on the ground floor of the main house, hosts an extensive collection of portraits of the Fairfax family, including an earlier Sir Thomas Fairfax, one of the leading generals in the Parliamentary army, during the English Civil War.

Catherine's oldest son was born at Leeds. He was also named Thomas Fairfax and bore the title 6th Lord Fairfax of Cameron. His story is quite remarkable. From the Culpepper family he inherited the rights to a vast swathe of land, known as the "Northern Neck Proprietary," totalling just under six million acres. In the 1730s he travelled to America to inspect his new possessions and eventually decided to give up Leeds Castle and to emigrate, which made him the only British Peer in America.

Thus the main branch of the family re-established themselves in the new world and were known to be friends of George Washington around 1745. Those who remained lacked the finances to properly care for the castle and the 7th Lord Fairfax died in poverty. Later the castle passed, by marriage and inheritance to the Wykeham Martin family. By now the whole place was in a bad state of disrepair, especially the mill, the gatehouse and the gloriette.

Fiennes Wykeham Martin has become a somewhat controversial figure in the history of the castle. He strongly disliked the Jacobean house, which had been modified, to a kind of mock-gothic style which was popular at the time of the Romantic Movement. He is said to have spent £30,000 on renovating the property, a considerable sum in 1822. He cleared the moat, repaired the walls of the gloriette, swept away many of the structures which had been added in the Tudor and Stuart periods, including the Jacobean house, and constructed a Mock-Tudor block in the middle bailey. He also lowered the main walls. This one act alone has had a profound impact on the appearance of the castle. Looking across the moat, from the stable block area, visitors can enjoy an idyllic panorama of the whole castle laid out before them, whereas in the medieval period the two circuits of high walls would have completely blocked that view. Leeds had made the metamorphosis from a defensive structure to a showpiece country house.

Whether Martin's changes were good or bad, the cost of them wiped out his finances, but fortunately his son Charles Wykeham Martin married a rich wife and made a good fortune of his own. The family continued to live at Hever until 1925, when the castle was purchased by a wealthy Anglo-American heiress, Mrs Wilson-Filmer, later known by the married name of Lady Baillie.

This new owner went to work with immense energy, making structural improvements to the main residential building, often described as the "new castle." She then brought in Armand-Albert Rateau, an immensely skilled expert in the Art-Deco style to complete the renovations. His work can be seen in the banqueting hall, the music room where the chapel had been, the staircase south of the fountain court, and much more besides. In short, Rateau updated the property to a 20th Century version of the charming Gothic Palace which it had always been.

As such it became the much loved destination of some of the most wealthy and fashionable personalities in 20th Century society. However it was also used as a hospital for airmen who had suffered from severe burns during the Second World War.

Bruce W. Johnson

Lady Baillie's will left the castle in the care of the Leeds Castle Charitable Foundation. In this, she was a visionary, safeguarding the castle for the enjoyment of future generations. The property is well known for hosting top level international conferences, but is also open to the public. It receives half a million visitors a year.

Having visited Leeds in November 2021, I returned just a year later to find that significant changes had been made to the displays being hosted in the main building. More emphasis is now being placed on the castle as it would have appeared in the lifetime of Lady Baillie, who rescued the site and restored its interior to create the spectacular building we see today. This change of emphasis is a bold move, but justified, in my opinion. A castle cannot be fixed in time. A document, such as Magna Carta, is unchanging, but a castle is constantly evolving and whatever we see, at Leeds or elsewhere, is really a collection of many layers of history, each one built upon those below. The only way to truly understand the story of Leeds is to see the final result, as it appeared in the middle of the Twentieth Century, nestling on top of the earlier layers in as much as they survive.

Lady Baillie's foresight in setting up the trust which manages the castle has rightly secured her place in its history. The interiors of the rooms could never be displayed in their medieval state. That was all swept away long ago. Instead we are treated to a Twentieth Century masterpiece in the arts of restoration and reconstruction. Any description must be peppered with superlatives. The library collection is breath-taking. The ceiling of the Servants' Hall is remarkable. The woodwork in the Thorpe Hall is magnificent and the door surrounds in the yellow drawing room are spectacular. I have not included photographs and I would not wish to. These are sights which all explorers must see for themselves.

The corridor which leads to the Gloriette is actually enclosed inside a stone bridge, making it possible to pass between the two without being shot at!

On the far side the visitor can experience first-hand the lifestyle of the 1920s and 1930s, in Lady Bailey's salon where distinguished guests would have talked fashion and politics beside the massive fireplace. The private writing room has magnificent views out over the lake, and a secret staircase by which her ladyship could ascend directly to her private rooms above. There is another staircase, magnificent in both its craftsmanship and its appearance. At the top we find ourselves exploring the boudoir, bathroom and bedroom of our host.

One of the bedrooms even serves to remind us of the political affairs which were developing beyond the safety of the castle, with a meeting table and despatch boxes. George Ambrose Lloyd, a member of Churchill's War Cabinet, was a frequent visitor to the house, which served, to some extent, as a country retreat for those who led Britain during the early days of the Second World War.

The structure and appearance of the keep itself is wonderfully contradictory; after seeing so many castles which are merely empty shells it is wonderful to see how this fortified building is lined with luxurious chambers, packed together around a small courtyard. It seems that, for once, one can truly understand how it was to live in a castle, and yet we must remind ourselves that all of this grandeur was installed in the first half of the twentieth century, at a time when the rest of the world was discovering movies and motor-cars.

Living in a castle
Leeds Castle has often been used for international conferences. Kings and Queens have relished experienced its tranquillity. Presidents and Prime ministers have experienced its charm. It is indeed a privilege to be able to enjoy its beauty as they have done. I have personally stayed at the castle on several occasions and was delighted with both the rooms and the service. It has a high quality restaurant with a stunning view of the castle.

Each room is different though all are of a very high standard. It is therefore advisable to book well in advance in order to enjoy a wider range of rooms and prices.

There are also a rich selection of special activities taking place throughout the year, including Concerts, Christmas celebrations, New-Year's Eve, Valentines Parties, Firework Displays and Halloween. [See the castle website]

Bed and breakfast accommodation is available on site, with a wide range of rooms and a price range to suit most budgets, although it tends to be booked well ahead. There are also holiday cottages, suitable for families, and for those on a more modest budget there is a camp site. There is also a high quality restaurant for evening meals and cafes for daytime snacks. [See the castle website for full details]

Wedding Venue
Leeds Castle was often given by kings of England as a gift to their wives, and has been associated with some very charismatic women. This element of romance has endured through the centuries. At the time of writing [2022] the Castle was available as a venue for various functions including high quality wedding receptions. See the castle's official website for details.

Bruce W. Johnson

Travel Note

There is more than one entrance to Leeds Estate. Satnav devices will generally lead you to the nearest one, which may not be the one you want. I suggest navigating first to a local restaurant, the Park Gate Inn, ME17 1PG.

For the day-visitors entrance head north, with the inn on your left, and take the first left turn into Penfold Hill.

For the bed-and breakfast accommodation, head south with the inn on your right, and take the first right into Broomfield Road.

Leybourne Castle

A minor structure near Maidstone. Privately owned
Postcode for Satnav: ME19 5HD
Nearest major road   M20 - A 228
Parking Arrangements: Park on roadside
Approaching from the motorway, take the next right turn after the Premiere Inn, or if driving towards the motorway, take the first left after St. Peter and St. Paul's Church. That road will bring you to the site, which is just 50 metres to the west of the church.

Also nearby:
Bradbourne House, historic manor house and wedding venue.

The remaining elements of Leybourne Castle have been incorporated into a more recent house which is on private land. You can only view the remains from the road, or from the church-yard. It is a most unusual arrangement and interesting to take a peek if you are passing but I would not recommend making a long journey just to see it.

History
After the Norman Conquest, the land at Leybourne was granted to William the Conqueror's half-brother, Bishop Odo of Bayeux. In the following century Sir Roger Leybourne built the stone castle in 1190, then went off to Palestine on crusade with Richard the Lionheart. When he died in 1198 the castle passed to his son, Roger Leybourne, Warden of the Cinque Ports.

Roger also went on crusade, in 1272, which is more than seventy years after his father's death. Obviously he must have been a very old man. An account published by the local church suggests that he probably had to drop out, en route, due to ill health, and died in France. His heart was embalmed and sent home and placed in the left hand casket of the Heart Shrine in the north wall of the local church, St. Peter and St. Paul. The right hand casket was never used. For many years this unique double shrine was obscured by rubble, and was rediscovered by Charles Hawley who was the local rector from 1877 - 1914. At this point the shrine was opened and found to contain a lead casket containing the remains of the heart.

Another member of the Leybourne family to be commemorated in the church is William (d. 1310), son of Sir Roger, who was the first Englishman to bear the title Admiral and was also the Constable of Pevensey Castle. . On 25th October 1286 King Edward and Queen Eleanor visited Sir William at Leybourne castle.

The last of the line was Juliana de Leybourne, who was married three times but never had an heir. On her death the castle passed to the crown.

Edward III granted it to the church, through the Cistercian Abbey of St. Mary's Graces. It was confiscated during the English reformation and had a number of owners, gradually falling into disrepair and being damaged by at least two fires. In 1930 the ruins were converted into a private house which still stands, a very unique situation.

The modern house is nestled between a gatehouse, which has two drum towers, and another tower to the south, there are also remains of what may have been a chapel or a feast hall. During the twentieth century it was still possible to explore two tunnels which ran under the site, but they have now been blocked off for safety reasons.

Castles of Kent

Lullingstone Castle and The World Garden

A major site between Swanley and Sevenoaks. Privately owned.
Postcode for Satnav: DA4 0JA
Nearest major road   M20 - A225
Website: https://www.lullingstonecastle.co.uk/
Parking Arrangements: On site
Public transport: Eynsford Railway Station

Also nearby
Lullingstone Roman Villa
Shoreham Castle
Eynsford Castle, DA4 0AA

Lullingstone Castle, the World Garden and Lullingstone Roman Villa, are all within just a minute's walk of one another, and it is well worthwhile to see them all in a single excursion. At the time of writing the castle site is only open during summer months, so check from the official website before planning your visit.

Lullingstone Castle: The Gatehouse

History

John de Rokesle owned the property until his death in 1361, when it passed to an alderman of the City of London called John Peche. One of his descendants built two splendid brick gatehouses, one of which still remains, an iconic legacy of Lullingstone's former splendour.

A later Sir John Peche, was a close friend and strong supporter of King Henry VII. He was a jousting champion, and at the age of 24 he fought at the Battle of Blackheath in 1497, being knighted afterwards for his efforts. He was appointed Sheriff of Kent and was responsible for escorting the pretender, Perkin Warbeck, as a prisoner to London.

Sir John Peche was appointed first Lieutenant of a troop of royal guards, known as the Band of Gentleman Pensioners. But before long these "gentlemen" were banned from the royal court as they were thought to be a "bad influence" on the King!

The next owner of Lullingstone was his nephew Sir Percival Hart, an interesting character who live to the ripe old age of 84, by which time he had served as "Knight Harbinger" to Henry VIII and all of his three children.

The building later passed, by marriage, to the Dyke family, with whom it still remains. They can trace their family lineage back to King Edward III.

Description

The iconic feature of the Lullingstone site is a magnificent Tudor gatehouse constructed in red brick and decorated with crenellations and octagonal towers.

The main house was reconstructed with a new façade in the reign of Queen Anne.

St. Botolph's Parish Church, on the castle lawn, features some of the oldest stained glass in England.

The World Garden

One of the fascinating attractions of Lullingstone is the profuse assemblage of plants from all corners of the world, to be found in the World Garden.

Lullingstone: The World Garden

The world garden project was conceived and initiated by Thomas Hart-Dyke and opened to the public in 2005. The amazing story behind its creation can be read on the Lullingstone Castle website.

Bruce W. Johnson

Lympne Castle

A major structure near Hythe. Privately owned
Postcode for Satnav: CT21 4LQ
Nearest major road   M20
Website: https://www.lympnecastle.com/
Parking Arrangements; on street

Also nearby
Port Lympne Safari Park
Crypt of St. Leonards Church, Hythe

Lympne Castle, c1900

History

Lympne Castle is fascinating by virtue of its historical position. Some say that the castle is the Roman fort knowns as Portus Lemanis, but in fact this is a slight misunderstanding.

The castle stands at the top of a cliff, and in Roman times the sea came almost to the foot of the cliff. Portus Lemanis was a harbour at the bottom of the cliff. After the fall of the Roman Empire the port declined and the remaining inhabitants gradually located to the area where a roman watchtower stood at the top of the cliff which would, perhaps, have given them greater safety from seaborne raiders. After the Norman Conquest the village and surrounding lands belonged to the church and a fortified manor house was built.

The old watchtower was included in the construction. The castle was enlarged to its present size around 1360, to protect against French raiders during the Hundred Years War.

Remarkably, even though the castle was church property, it was not taken over by the king at the time of the English Reformation but remained the property of the Archdeacons of Canterbury Cathedral.

By 1800 the property was in a bad state of disrepair and was being used as a farmhouse. In 1860 it was sold by the church. In 1905 it was purchased by a Mr. Tennent who set about restoring it and built a new wing.

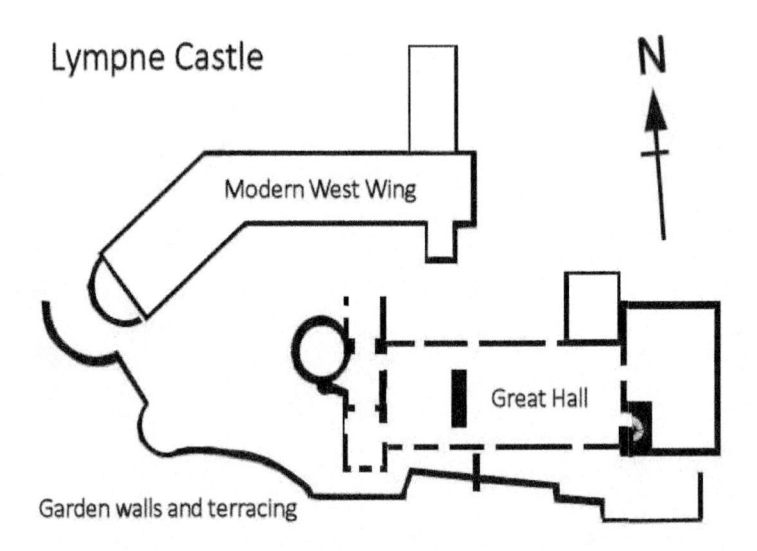

Lympne Castle

N

Modern West Wing

Great Hall

Garden walls and terracing

Description and Defences

Approaching Lympne by road, the small village and its parish church have a slightly gloomy, very gothic atmosphere which many people, including myself, find both fascinating and attractive. Once within the walls of the castle there is a total change of mood as the interior is beautifully decorated, still in keeping with a medieval castle but bright and inviting.

The Great Hall, at the centre of the property, is an imposing building, with part panelled walls, wooden roof beams and gothic arched windows.

The Drawing Room, in the west wing, was added in Edwardian times by the famous architect Sir Robert Lorimer. It is tastefully decorated with Wood panelling and a stone fireplace. The bay window offers panoramic views towards the south east coast.

From the castle there is an excellent view out over the farming fields below, and it is possible to see the remains of Stutfall Castle which was the original Roman Fort Portus Lemanis, about 500 meters to the south-west.

Lympne Castle as viewed from Stutfall

To view the castle from the south, one can travel along the Royal Military Road to West Hythe Dam, postcode CT21 4NS. This gives you an excellent view with the additional option of walking up to Stutfall Castle at CT21 4LQ and getting an even closer view from there.

In recent years the Castle has been in use as a high quality wedding venue and there are also a number of holiday cottages. Details are given on the castle's own website.

Mereworth Castle

A significant site near Maidstone. Privately owned.
Postcode for Satnav: ME18 5JB
Nearest major road   M20 - A228

    This site is referred to as a castle because the original building was a fortified manor house with a licence to crenellate dating back to 1332. The present building, however, is not really a castle at all, but has immense architectural importance, nevertheless.

Mereworth, detail from a print by Neale.

    Andrea Palladio [b.1508 - d.1580] was an Italian architect of the renaissance period. He designed city mansions, country villas and churches, all of which featured the classical styles of the Greeks and Romans which were revisited in the renaissance. These features included the classic rectangular lines, rectangular windows, domes, and columns which we generally associate with Greek temples and Roman forums. Two outstanding examples of his work are the Villa Capra and the Villa Rotunda. Palladio never came to Britain, but the English architect, Inigo Jones went to Italy twice between 1598 and 1606. He was heavily influenced by the neo-classical style as can be seen from the Banqueting House in Whitehall, which he designed for King James I

Mereworth is perhaps the best and most famous example we have in England of a Palladian villa, another being Chiswick House in Middlesex. It was not designed by Jones himself, but by one of his disciples, Colen Campbell, for John Fane, Earl of Westmorland.

The Palladian style itself did not become widespread in England, mainly because it wasn't so well suited to British weather, but it was the precursor of the Georgian style, which became its legacy.

Should you, even for a moment, wish to consider just how influential Mereworth was, just compare it to the United States Capitol Building, or to the National Gallery and Saint Paul's Cathedral in London.

In that context, Mereworth is a very beautiful and significant piece of architecture, just not a castle as we would expect from the name.

Old Soar Manor House

A minor site near Sevenoaks. Owned by English Heritage and administered by the National Trust.
Postcode for Satnav: TN15 0QX
Nearest major road   A25
Website
https://www.english-heritage.org.uk/visit/places/old-soar-manor/

Also nearby
Ightham Mote TN15 0NT

Description and Defences
   Old Soar is a medieval manor house, much of which has been demolished.
   Open to visit in the summer months only. At the time of writing the visits were free of charge. Check the official website for current details.

Bruce W. Johnson

Otford Palace

A major structure near Sevenoaks.
Managed by the Archbishop's Palace Conservation Trust
Postcode for Satnav: TN14 5PG
Nearest major road M26
Website: https://otfordpalace.org/
Parking Arrangements: On street or Otford Village Car Park.
Public transport: Otford Railway Station

History

From 790 onwards there is a long history of lands at Otford being bequeathed to Christ Church, Canterbury, beginning with a certain Offa, King of Mercia who gifted the actual village.

As the estate grew, a large moated manor house was constructed. It was to be church property for the next 600 years.

In 1066 William the Conqueror rested at Otford on his march from Hastings to London. As listed in the Domesday survey of 1086 the estate was large enough to include six water-mills, an indicator of how much cereal was being harvested. Some of the wealth this generated was used to construct a fine dwelling house for the Archbishop of Canterbury, who used it as a country estate. Robert Winchelsey, Archbishop of Canterbury, had a grand new chapel, 60 feet long, constructed in the decorated style

In 1326 it was used as a place of safety by Archbishop Reynolds when the London mob killed Walter Stapledon, the Bishop of Exeter, and in 1348 Edward III moved his court to Otford to avoid the Black Death.

The Great Hall was completed around 1513. Being 103 feet long and 40 feet wide it was considered to be able to seat 200 at dinner, and as seen now in its restored form it provides a fantastic example of a medieval interior.

In 1514 King Henry and his sister, Princess Mary stayed overnight at Otford Palace on their way to Dover, where Mary took ship to marry the King of France.

William Warham was the last Roman Catholic Archbishop of Canterbury. He spent lavishly on reconstructing the palace at Otford, creating a residence so luxurious that Henry VIII and Catherine of Aragon used it as an overnight lodging en-route to the Field of Cloth of Gold.

Archbishop Cranmer began work on his Book of Common Prayer at the Palace. It is believed that he finished this work before he left.

Henry VIII took possession of the palace on the 1st of January 1537. He spent even more money on it, and his daughter Mary Tudor stayed there as a girl.

In time, however, he came to prefer Knole House in Sevenoaks. After Henry's death, the Palace fell gradually into disrepair.

Queen Elizabeth I stayed at the palace during her Royal Progress in 1559. A survey by her staff found that there were 200 door keys missing, which gives some indication of the sheer size of the place. In any case, the Queens staff discouraged her from staying at Otford as it was very damp due to underground water systems in the area. Eventually, Elizabeth sold off the property to Sir Robert Sydney.

Otford Palace

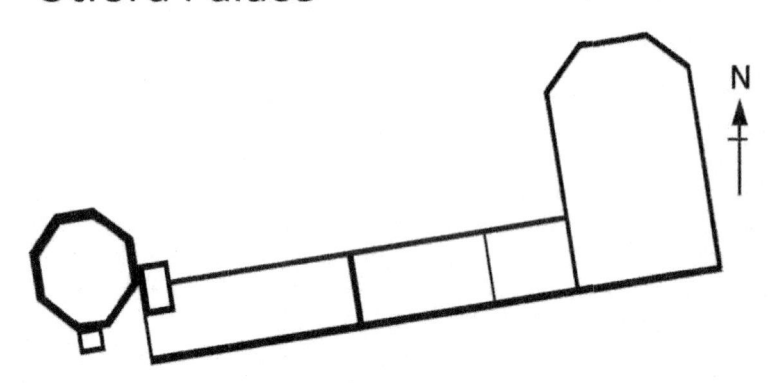

As with so many such sites, Otford declined over the following centuries and was eventually reduced to being used as a farmhouse. Following the death of Harry Wellband, a highly successful Otford farmer and agricultural contractor, Castle Farm was sold in 1933.

In 1973 a local builder began to work on the site, and this led to some excavations taking place.

By 2016 the remaining buildings were so dangerous that Sevenoaks district council had to carry out repairs.

In 2017 a conservation trust was formed to restore and preserve what remained of the Archbishop's Palace and promote public education concerning it history. The trust's registration number is 1173486. They appear to have done a magnificent job in repairing and presenting the palace. Models and visual graphics of the site can help us to visualise its former glory. Without any doubt it was a highly significant structure.

The Palace is scheduled under the Ancient Monuments and Archaeological Areas Act (1979). List entry number 1005197.

Bruce W. Johnson

Penshurst Place

A major structure near Tonbridge. Privately owned
Postcode for Satnav: TN11 8DG
Nearest major road   A21 / A26
Website: https://www.penshurstplace.com/
Parking Arrangements: On site
Public transport: Leigh or Fleur de Lis railway stations are the closest, but still more than a mile to walk or cycle.

Also nearby
Chiddingstone Village [National Trust]

History

The manor house at Penshurst was owned by Sir John Pulteney, Lord Mayor of London, who expanded the main building, but died of the Black Death in 1349, and so had precious little time to enjoy his new construction. Penshurst passed to Sir John Deveraux and then to John Duke of Bedford and Humphrey Duke of Gloucester, who were the brothers of King Henry V, the victor of Agincourt.

Later, in the reign of Henry VIII, another Humphrey owned the castle. Humphrey Stafford was the 1st Duke of Buckingham. Following his execution in 1521 the house was taken by the crown. Edward VI gifted it to Sir William Sidney, and the house was the birthplace of the Elizabethan courtier, Sir Phillip Sidney. It has been passed on by inheritance since that time and is still owned by a family member, the Viscount De L' Isle.

Description and Defences

Sir John Deveraux was granted a licence to crenellate the buildings in 1392. He had a curtain wall constructed around the property with towers at the corners and two gatehouses, on the north and south sides. Most of the fortifications were taken down when it was felt that they were no longer needed. One of the towers, known as the Garden Tower, still remains.

As a stately home, the remaining buildings are of excellent quality, and benefit from the beautifying effects of the creamy coloured sandstone. Many stages of demolition and redevelopment have taken place but the original medieval hall remains the central core of the house. The wooden roof alone is a masterful work of art, constructed from chestnut, rather than oak. I was informed by a member of the staff that this timber work was carried out by king's own craftsmen, sent down to Kent as a favour to do the work. In the centre of the room stands a huge wrought iron fire place, a legacy of medieval times when there was no chimney.

Penshurst Place: The Great Hall, by Nash

This drawing of the great hall, by Nash, shows the residents of Penshurst enjoying a celebration. The picture includes the timbered roof and the central fire-hearth.

The artist, Joseph Nash, lived from 1808 to 1878. His most famous work was a 4-volume set entitled "Mansions of England in the Olden Time," published from 1839–49. It is important to realise that this is an artist's impression produced in the Victorian era, and may not be an entirely true reflection of how the residents lived in the medieval period.

The remaining rooms are sumptuous and spectacular, with a superlative range of high quality collections including furniture, antique weapons, fine china, and, of course, fine art.

The exquisite gardens provide another attraction, and there is also a very good toy museum on site, which appeals to children of all ages.

One would rarely include the gift shop or the café among the attractions of such an important historical site, but The "Porcupine Pantry" at Penshurst is something exceptional. As a combined gift shop and café, offering a rich variety of both refreshments and souvenirs, it really is a treat in itself. On one recent visit we bought a very nice squirrel house for our garden.

Penshurst Place from an engraving by J.P. Neale c1823

At the time of writing [2022] the facilities were available for corporate events and as a high quality wedding venue, see the official website for details.

Queenborough Castle

A redeveloped site on the Isle of Sheppey.
Postcode for Satnav: ME11 5AS
Nearest major road: A249
Public Transport: Sheerness Railway Station

Also nearby;
Sheerness Guildhall Museum

In its time Queenborough Castle was perhaps the most perfect piece of military engineering ever constructed in this country. Now, nothing at all remains, neither ditch nor stone, not even a shadow of its lost grandeur.

I have included it in this gazetteer in order to preserve its memory but there really is very little see at this location and I would not advise making a long journey to visit the site. In 2010 Kent County Council discussed a plan to mark the outlines of the walls with flowering bulbs, an indication of just how completely the actual structures have disappeared. Fortunately these outlines do show up well in satellite images.

History
Queenborough Castle was constructed at Sheerness on the Isle of Sheppey between 1361 and 1377. It was a royal castle, built for the defence of the realm, and not intended to be the home of an aristocrat, although both Henry III and Edward III liked to visit.

This was the period of the Hundred Years War, and although most of the battles were fought in France, it was always possible that the French would raid the English coast. The town of Sheerness had an obvious strategic value. Its position on the Isle of Sheppey gives it control of the River Medway, but also allows it to intercept any enemy fleet which might attempt to enter the mouth of the Thames.

In fact, the French never attacked Queenborough, and it was only besieged once. In 1450 there was a popular rebellion led by Jack Cade, which originated in Sussex and spread out into Kent. The rebel numbers were not huge, perhaps 5000 men in all, but the authorities underestimated their determination and the rebels won a victory at Sevenoaks in June 1450, then marched towards London.

John Cokeram, the Mayor of Queenborough and some of the townsmen led a section of the rebels in an attack on the castle, but they were driven off by the Constable of the castle and his small garrison force.

When the rebels reached London they began looting which led to the citizens of London turning out in force and a bloody battle took place on London Bridge. The King offered a pardon to the rebels if they agreed to go home. This left Cade without an army, and on the 12th of July he had been captured, mortally wounded, and had died before coming to trial. Thus the rebellion failed and the men who had attacked Queenborough Castle were ultimately executed.

The castle continued to be important in the Tudor era. Henry VIII had plenty of enemies, including France, Spain and the Roman Catholic Church. He was constantly concerned about the risk of foreign invasion and he spent money upgrading Queenborough, as did Queen Elizabeth I, for the same reasons.

The castle served as a stronghold for the Royalists during the English Civil War, and as a result it was demolished by order of Parliament in 1650 when the war was over. Most of the materials were either sold or robbed by the local people. In retrospect this was a mistake by the authorities as it made it possible for the Dutch to raid the Medway area in the war of 1667. Said by some to be the greatest castle in England, nothing at all remains of it now, though in aerial photographs it is sometimes possible to see patterns on the grass.

Description and Defences

The castle was designed and its construction managed by Henry Yevele [1320 - 1400] who served as master mason to King Edward III and is known for the high quality of his work on Canterbury Cathedral including the Nave and the Chapter House.

Queenborough Castle, detail from a work by Hooper c1783

Note the tall, square gatehouse tower at the rear of ther sketch, which is not so obvious when looking at the plan view.

The castle was built on a slight mound which may originally have been a pre-historic structure. The actual mound is still visible just across the road from Queenborough Station. Nothing remains of the defences, however it is worth taking a look at images of the site taken with aerial photography as the outlines of the fort tend to show up as patterns in the grass, depending on the time of year. Based on these patterns and on antique prints, we can see that the design was unique and very much ahead of its time, resembling the artillery forts of the Tudor period.

Queenborough Castle

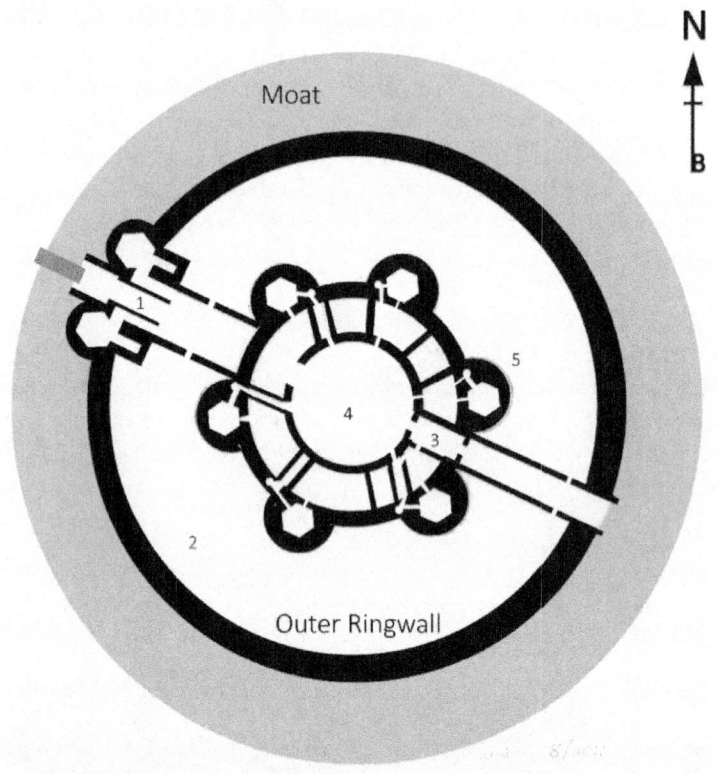

1 Outer Gatehouse
2 Outer Bailey
3 Inner Gatehouse
4 Inner Bailey
5 Towers

The first line of defence was the wet ditch, or moat. There were then two concentric lines of walls, both perfectly circular, and strongly built to resist siege weapons. The gatehouse was on the west side. If the enemy managed to break through the outer gates they would then have to run right round the bailey yard under fire from all sides in order to attack the inner gatehouse which was on the east side. The inner wall had six massive circular towers equally spaced along it.

Queenborough, therefore, was what is called a "Concentric Fort." In fact it could be described as the ultimate in concentric forts and this has caused some problems for military historians.

Low-built concentric forts are generally associated with the years after 1400 when large cannon were coming into use. Cannons were best against wooden ships when firing from water level, or at least as close as possible. It is as if Queenborough had been designed as fort for cannon, but in the years before cannon were being used. Various experts have argued about this, but I suspect that they have allowed themselves to be distracted. Just because the outer wall is low, that does not imply it was built for cannon. By having a high inner wall and a lower outer wall it was possible for archers to shoot from both walls at the same time. Furthermore, if an enemy had gained access to the outer walls, the defenders would still have had the advantage of shooting down on them from the higher walls inside.

The central area was a keep with six separate towers, and again, the enemy would be under constant fire from all sides whilst attempting to force an entry.

Reculver Roman Fort

A major structure near Herne Bay: English Heritage
Postcode for Satnav: CT6 6SS
Nearest major road   A299
Website: English-Heritage.org.uk
Parking Arrangements: Public carpark
Public transport: Herne Bay railway station 4 miles.

Also nearby
The Spitfire and Hurricane Memorial Museum, CT12 5DF

Description and Defences

Roman camps and forts were generally laid out in a pattern which resembles a playing card, that is, a rectangle with rounded corners, and a gate midway along each of the four sides. Good examples of these can be seen at Hadrian's Wall in the north of England. At Reculver the fort was almost a square, being 570 ft. by 585 ft. but it still featured the rounded corners.

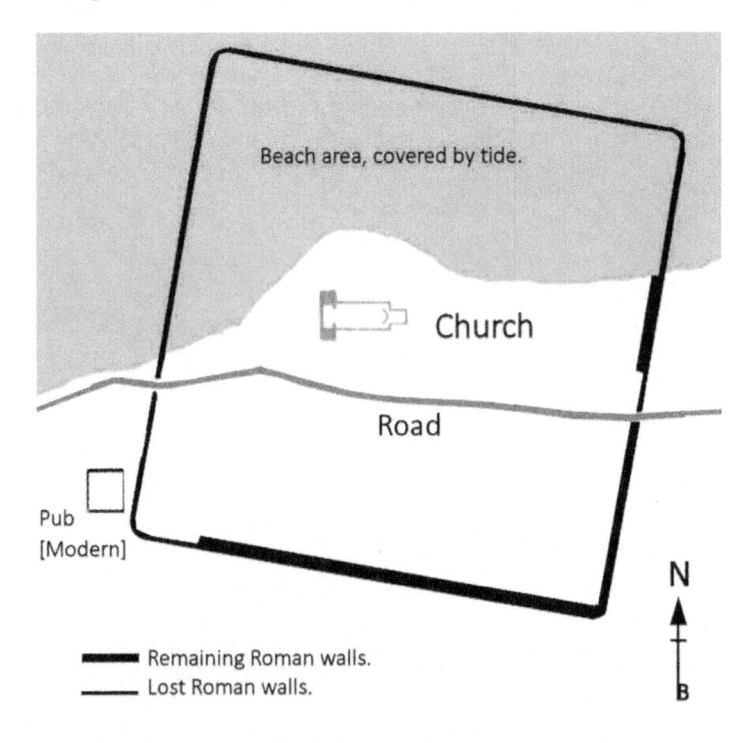

Reculver Roman Station

Originally there would have been a wall ten feet thick at the bottom and 8 ft. further up, with a ditch and an earth rampart in front. This was a standard arrangement at most Roman defensive works. Some of the wall sections are still visible, especially in the area behind the local pub, currently known as the King Ethelbert.

History

The Roman camp at Reculver marked a significant position on the Kent coast, nine miles from Canterbury.

The Blean Forest is an area of low hills, spreading out from central Kent, between the Thames Valley and the south coast. Their most westerly spur forms a slight ridge, just 50 ft. above sea level. In Roman times it would have been almost an island, with marshes to the west and sea on the other three sides, the last piece of the mainland before the Isle of Thanet.

The Roman Fort was named Regulbium and was constructed in the second century, when the Romans had already been in England for around a hundred years. It was therefore a feature of the peacetime occupation, not the conquest.

The fort was not actually built on the coast, rather the sea has eaten away the land which once lay to the north of it. Even as recently as 1530 Leland described it as being a quarter of a mile back from the sea. It therefore seems likely that it had been built on the firm ground of the ridge, perhaps controlling a small river which led inland.

From its geographical position we would assume that its function was to guard and patrol the sea routes as trade developed between Britain and the continent. As time passed its function changed. In the third and fourth centuries the Roman colony was increasingly menaced by Anglo Saxon raiders and Reculver became part of the defensive network which was known as "The Forts of the Saxon Shore."

Thus we can say that for the Romans the fort had a treble value. It guarded the approaches to the Thames, it provided a base for patrolling the channel and it stood watch against any barbarians who might seek to use the Isle of Thanet as a base.

The twin towers are the most impressive feature of the site, but they are not part of the Roman fort at all. By 669 A.D. the Romans were long gone and the Saxons had accepted Christianity. England was dominated by the Anglo-Saxons, although Kent itself had been settled by a people known as the Jutes, from Jutland, which we now call Denmark. It is likely that the old walls of the Roman camp now protected a small town.

In 690 King Egbert [or Ecgbehrt] of Kent founded a "Minster" built in the ruins of the Roman fortress and utilising the stones of the Roman buildings. Records suggest that many of the clergy installed there were foreign

Christians from as far away as Turkey, Syria and North Africa, possibly refugees from the Muslim jihad.

By the ninth century the monastery had become very wealthy, but after that it declined as it was too easy a target for Viking invaders who are known to have landed on both the Isle of Thanet and the Isle of Sheppey. At least one monk, known as Ymar, was made a saint after being slain by the Northmen.

By 1200 the building was probably a parish church, rather than a monastery. In any case, the Christian Church was so powerful that military leaders avoided attacking it in any way and the local community at Reculver grew rich again. As a demonstration of wealth the church was enlarged and a new west-front was added including two large towers which became a local landmark, used a lot by coastal shipping to identify their position on the coast.

Writing in 1540 John Leyland referred to an ornate stone cross, nine feet high, which stood in the choir of the church, describing it as the "fairest and most ancient cross that I ever saw."

Old Saint Mary's Church, Reculver, before its destruction.

During the next two centuries the sea began to erode the coastline, drawing ever closer to the walls of the old Roman fort. Then in 1807 a major storm led to the sea reaching within 30 feet of the walls. A meeting was held, locally, to agree a programme of sea defences, and church repairs. Unexpectedly the meeting was hijacked by the brash young vicar, Christopher Naylor, egged on by his mother. Naylor proposed that the ancient Anglo-Saxon site should be demolished. With little further consideration the building was blown apart using gunpowder and two thousand tons of stone were sold off and used to build Margate Pier.

Trinity House bought the two towers for £100 and repaired them so that they could continue to be used as a navigational landmark, but the rest of the building has been lost forever. The great Saxon cross was destroyed with the rest, and its fragments are now kept in Canterbury Cathedral.

In terms of our national heritage this was an absolute catastrophe. Many ancient monasteries had been destroyed in the English Reformation and the Puritan Revolution, but here was an ecclesiastic treasure with elements dating right back to Roman times, perhaps the oldest surviving church in the whole of the British Isles, and it was blown to pieces in an act of vandalism and stupidity.

In 1966 several months of Archaeological excavations were completed under the supervision of the Ministry of Works, and reported in the Kent Archaeological Review. The dig had uncovered the remains of eleven infants, none of them more than a few months of age. They were found in an area on the western side of the fort, close to where the pub now stands. Most of the bodies could be dated to the Roman period, but one was medieval. It is not possible to fully determine the circumstances of these burials, however the bodies had been buried with certain ritual details and there were suggestions that human sacrifice may have taken place during the pre-Christian period. If the site was known to have a lasting connection with pagan ritual that could, perhaps, explain why the church was built, in order to sanctify the land. We must be careful, however, and avoid jumping to conclusions. It is equally possible that this was merely a graveyard for infants who had not been baptised into the Catholic Church and therefore could not be buried on consecrated ground.

Richborough Castle

A major structure near Sandwich. English Heritage
Postcode for Satnav: CT13 9JW
Nearest major road   A256
Website: https://www.english-heritage.org.uk/visit/places/richborough-roman-fort-and-amphitheatre/
Parking Arrangements: Small car park next to site entrance.
Public transport: Sandwich railway station - a mile and a half.

Also nearby
Richborough Roman Amphitheatre
Sandwich village
Saint Augustine's Cross, CT12 5JB
Viking Ship Hugin at Cliffsend, near Ramsgate.

History
    Julius Caesar conducted a short mission to Britain in 55 B.C. but the real Roman invasion did not take place until 43 A.D. In the reign of the Emperor Claudius the Roman general Aulus Plautius led a full scale invasion with four complete legions and their support troops.
    To put that in context, there were only around 28 legions in the entire Roman Empire at this time. This was a significant force of about 40,000 men. They landed at Richborough which the Romans called Rutupiae. The Isle of Thanet really was an island at that time, so it provided them with a relatively safe haven while the troops and their animals were ferried over in three separate divisions.
    When their forces were assembled the Romans marched west, fighting a battle at the River Medway and capturing London. They then marched towards Colchester, capital of the Catauvellauni tribe.
    At this point the Emperor Claudius arrived from the continent to lead the army in person. He brought a number of elephants with him. Historians are quick to say that these animals would have terrified the British warriors, but that is just an assumption. The real point is that the Britons' elite troops were charioteers, and the elephants would have rendered them useless by causing panic among the horses. The Catauvellauni surrendered and 11 British kings submitted themselves to Roman rule.
    The successful campaign helped to solidify the position of Claudius as Roman Emperor, and provided the basis for the ongoing conquest of England and Wales.

Bruce W. Johnson

Richborough was used as a Roman supply depot, with defensive banks and ditches. A Roman road, Watling Street, was constructed from the Kent coast to London.

Around 85 A.D. the site was cleared and a huge monument, probably a triumphal arch, was erected to commemorate the Roman victory. Its foundations still remain. Around this area the town of Rutupiae grew to a size of around 21 hectares. As the first Roman port in Britain it would have enjoyed a considerable degree of prosperity. An amphitheatre was built nearby to provide entertainment.

Richborough Roman Fort

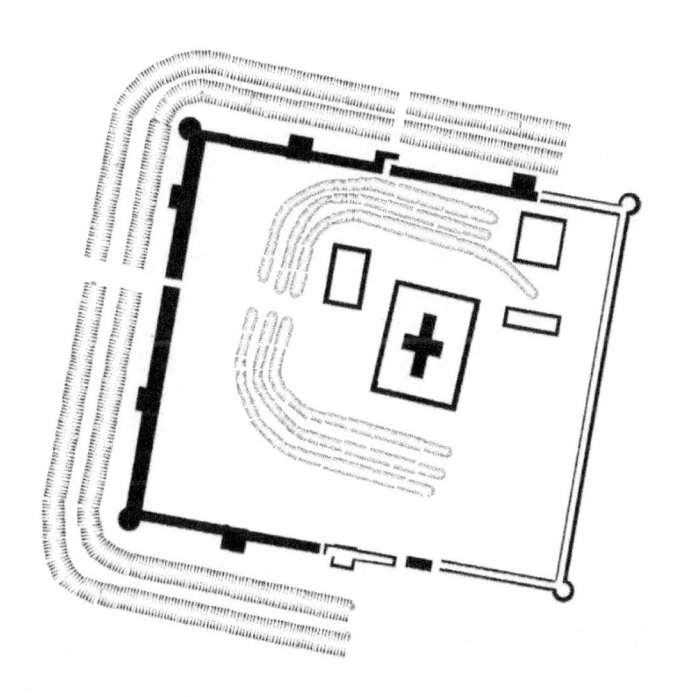

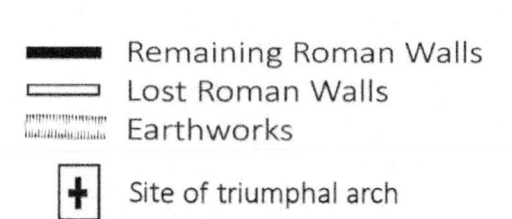

— Remaining Roman Walls
▭ Lost Roman Walls
▨ Earthworks
✚ Site of triumphal arch

N / B

Castles of Kent

In 287 A.D. a rebel general, Carausius, declared himself Emperor of Britain. The fort was rebuilt in stone and brick to protect against attack by the forces of the legitimate emperor. After the murder of Carausius in 293 the Emperor Constantinus Chlorus recaptured Britain without actually attacking Richborough.

In the years which followed the port seems to have been more prosperous than ever, and was regarded as the most important of those defences known as "The Forts of the Saxon Shore." This was a defensive system of fortified ports manned by both infantry and warships, under the command of an individual known as "The Count of the Saxon Shore," from the Latin "*comes littoris Saxonici per Britanniam.*"

Some writers have suggested the "Seat Perilous" referred to in the Arthurian legend is a reference to this office.

There are at least nine Roman forts which were part of this system, and four of them are in Kent; Reculver, [Regulbium] Richborough, [Rutupiae] Dover, [Dubris] and Stutfal Castle at Lympne [Portus Lemainis.]

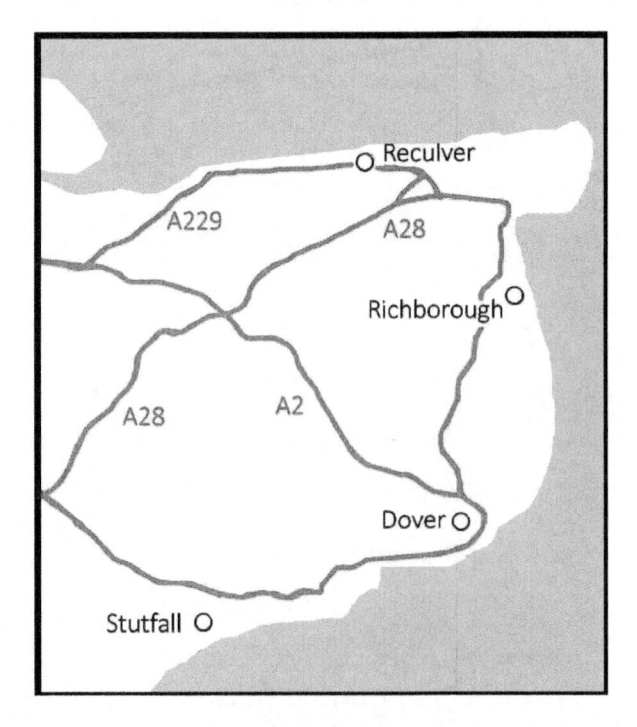

It is only fair to acknowledge that historians have different views about the reasons why these castles were built, with some suggesting they were intended as a defence against the Romans by the rebel Emperor Carausius.

This may be so, but as the years passed the forts were definitely put to use as bastions to hold back invaders from Europe.

Description and Defences

Studies of Richborough have not been easy work. The original settlement was built in a marshy area some distance back from the coast. Over the centuries the site has been damaged by both erosion and silting up. About one third of the fort is missing and that which still exists was built over earlier roman buildings. All of this has created challenges for the archaeologists.

The walls of the fortress were constructed from a mixture of small flint stones, brick tiles, rubble and mortar, which reflects the lack of good building stone in an area which stands mainly on chalk. It is estimated that the walls would have been around 30 feet high. Most Roman forts, like those on Hadrian's Wall, are laid out in a generic, rectangular pattern which is often described as "playing card shaped." The gate on the north wall is smaller than the others and its passage turns at a right angle. Excavations conducted in 2020 suggest that this connected to a narrow causeway which crossed a marshy area leading to the waterfront. In effect, a pedestrian gate leading down to the dockside.

Rochester Castle

A major structure in Rochester: English Heritage
Postcode for Satnav: ME1 1QE
Nearest major road   A2
Website: https://www.english-heritage.org.uk/visit/places/rochester-castle/
Parking Arrangements: Short term parking is available on the Esplanade, directly outside the Castle.
For longer term parking there are several sites just off the High Street:
Rochester Riverside Parking ME1 1PZ
Rochester Railway car park ME1 1NH
Blue Boar Car Park ME1 1PD
Public transport: Rochester Railway Station, 2 minute walk.

Also nearby;
Rochester Cathedral
Gundulf's Tower, [See earlier entry in this book]
Rochester Guildhall Museum ME1 1PY
Eastgate House ME1 1HS
Eastgate Gardens
Six Poor Travellers
Huguenot Museum
Rochester Art Gallery
War Memorial

History
There was a wall around the city of Durobrivae [Rochester] in Roman times, but the Normans chose to build their first motte and bailey castle on a small mound called Boley Hill, just up-river from the town. This holding, like many others in Kent, was granted to William the Conqueror's half-brother, Bishop Odo. He was a rather truculent character who managed to get himself banished from England by William.

Later, having been allowed back, he rebelled against the next king William Rufus, and the castle at Rochester was captured after a short siege in 1088. William Rufus must have recognised the strategic value of the castle because he gave orders to the next Bishop to build a new castle in stone. This time they decided to build the castle in one corner of the Roman town walls, just as they did with the Tower of London. In both cases the castles served a multiple purpose; to control the river and the road bridge which crossed it as well as controlling the local townsfolk. In 1127 work began on a huge keep, which was completed around 1139.

Rochester Castle: The Keep and Curtain Wall with Towers.

Traces of the early walls can still be seen on the Esplanade and perhaps in some of the garden walls on Castle Street.

By 1215 Rochester had become a royal castle, directly controlled by the king. These were troubled times. King John was constantly forced to deal with rebellions by his barons and in 1215 a knight named William de Albini seized the castle for the rebel side, with the aim of blocking the road between London and Dover. King John's men arrived within days, before the rebels could build up a large force at the site, and the king himself began to direct siege operations from October 13th.

History has sometimes portrayed King John as cowardly, weak and lethargic. Some historians fell that he has had a bad press because he was often in conflict with the church and the monks were the ones who wrote the history books. Whatever the truth of that matter, John certainly showed plenty of energy and determination in the way he conducted the siege of Rochester Castle. His plan of attack was entirely as would be expected. He used engineers and labourers to tunnel under the curtain wall at the point which was closest to the keep. The tunnel was supported with strong timbers. When the "mine" beneath the wall was big enough he had it filled with brushwood and animal fat, which was all set on fire. The supports were burned and the wall above collapsed.

The rebel knights fell back to defend the keep, but King John's men carried on mining and using the same techniques as before they were able to bring down one of the corner towers.

Even now the rebels continued to fight, withdrawing into the north-eastern half of the keep. No reinforcements arrived, however, and at last the rebels, having eaten their horses for food, were forced to surrender. The siege of 1215 was used as the basis for a feature film, called Ironclad, released in 2011 and featuring Brian Cox, Derek Jacobi and Charles Dance.

The damage to the keep was eventually repaired in the reign of Henry III. Soon after it came under attack by another group of rebellious barons, led this time by Simon De Montfort, however this time the action was short-lived and the rebels retreated without capturing the buildings.

One corner of the keep had been destroyed and had to be replaced, but the way in which this was done is fascinating. The old corner tower had been square in design. The new one was round, on the outside, to give greater strength, but was disguised at the top to make it look the same as the others when viewed from afar. Other signs of the rebuilding can be seen in the internal stonework, especially where a fireplace has been repaired. The curtain wall was also repaired.

Around 1360 the outer walls were strengthened with defensive towers in order to safeguard against an attack by the French. The sections which remain along the Esplanade are up to fifty feet high and would have had a river running directly below, creating a very strong defensive position.

The Peasant's Revolt took place in 1381. It was quite a local affair, involving mainly the agricultural labourers of Essex and Kent. Rochester Castle witnessed some hostilities but was in little danger of being captured.

In Tudor times the outer walls and buildings of the castle were used as a source of building materials for other projects, such as Upnor Castle on the other side of the Medway. This may seem short sighted and wasteful, but by now that time it was perceived that the real threats to the south east were expected to come up the river in ships, not marching up the road from Dover. This destruction continued in the Stuart period when Sir Anthony Weldon stripped the keep of all its building materials. He even tried to demolish it for building stone, but gave up as the keep was still so massive and strong that taking it down was costing too much.

The local council, Rochester Corporation, bought the castle in 1884 and turned the bailey yard into a park for the recreational use of citizens. In 1964 it was transferred to the Department of the Environment and in due course to English Heritage.

The present main entrance to the castle grounds is a nineteenth century alteration, but it is believed that there was a gatehouse there in medieval times, enabling passengers to alight from boats, which in those days could sail right up to the castle walls.

The main entrance to the bailey would have been in the eastern corner opening onto Castle Hill, which takes a sharp turn at that point, just opposite "Two Post Alley." The gatehouse from that entrance has been demolished.

In recent times a new entrance was dug through the walls at ground level, an act which some of us may regard as sheer vandalism. Fortunately, thanks to work done by English heritage, the true entrance is now back in use.

Description and Defences

We are fortunate to find that Rochester has retained both its keep and its curtain walls, complete with towers. All too often the outlying walls around a castle have been destroyed and only the keep remains. This gives a false impression of how large the original structure was. At Rochester we really can appreciate the original layout, with the massive keep standing proudly within the expansive bailey yard.

With walls fully twelve feet thick, the keep at Rochester is said to be the tallest in England, at 30.8 meters, plus turrets of 3.65 meters, a total of around 35.5 Meters all told. I would suggest that visitors will appreciate it all the more if they also visit Castle Hedingham in Essex, which gives some idea of the atmosphere which existed inside such a structure when complete with roof and floors.

One very important feature of the keep is the barbican, or entrance tower, which protects the actual doorway of the keep. This was a new, state of the art, feature when it was built. The weakest point of any structure is the entrance and any normal door could eventually be knocked down with a battering ram. To reach the door of Rochester Keep an attacker would have had to force their way into the fore-building and fight their way up a steep staircase. It would simply not be possible to get a battering ram up the stairs and round the corner, and there were also the problems of getting past a drawbridge and a portcullis.

Internally, the keep is divided in two by a cross-wall. This feature proved its value in 1215, when King John's men captured the south west side of the keep but the rebel knights managed to hang on in the north-eastern half of the building. There is also a well at the bottom with a shaft built into the stonework so that it can be accessed from all of the levels above. The lowest levels of the keep would have been used for storage, however there is also a small "postern" gate making it possible to exit onto the outer walls of the castle. It is easy to imagine this would be used for guardsmen to go out on patrol, but I think this is unlikely. The only essential reason I can imagine for such a door is as an emergency entrance, for men to get into the keep if the outer walls had been taken.

The three top floors are well decorated with Norman style stonework, such as dog-tooth mouldings and zig-zag tiling. There are two fireplaces on each level and plenty of garde-robe toilets. In peacetime the middle levels would have been used for a range of everyday activities ranging from feasts to administration. The top floor would have been the living quarters for the commander and his family and would have been known as the "Solar" because the windows were larger to let in more light.

Rochester Castle: The interior of the keep.

The floors are linked by two spiral staircases which allow modern visitors access all the way to the top. From the parapet one has an excellent view over the city and the River Medway.

Whilst out on the parapet, it is worth taking note of the small, regular holes around the inside of the walls. As a young schoolteacher I used to take parties of schoolchildren to visit the castle and the guides used to tell us that these were "pigeon holes" where pigeons were encouraged to live, in order to be used as a source of fresh food. I have since heard other opinions that these holes were to support the timbers which held up the roof. Perhaps it was a bit of both. I shall leave the readers to form their own opinions when they visit.

Information for visitors

Rochester High Street benefits from a number of important cultural and historical buildings, many of which have connections to Charles Dickens who grew up in the area. So, for example, Eastgate House is a grade 1 listed

Elizabethan building which features as Westgate in The Pickwick Papers and as the Nun's House in The Mystery of Edwin Drood. Now a Dickens Museum, the grounds of Eastgate House contain the Swiss chalet in which Dickens penned several of his novels. This is but one of many attractions which are worth viewing in addition to the castle. There is also a Dickens Festival each year.

Saltwood Castle

A major site near Hythe. Privately owned and not open to the public.
Postcode for Satnav: CT21 4QU
Nearest major road   M20
Website: https://www.saltwoodcastle.com/
Parking Arrangements
Public transport:

Also nearby
Crypt of St. Leonard's Church, Hythe. CT21 5DN
Westenhanger Castle CT21 4HX
Brockhill Country Park CT21 4HL
Lympne Castle
Port Lympne Safari Park and Dinosaur Forest.

Saltwood Castle is a most impressive medieval stronghold, located in the delightfully English town of Hythe. The castle is privately owned and not normally open to the public, although the Lady owner has sometimes been known to host open days and charity events in the summer months.

Sections of the curtain wall are visible from outside and the main entrance can be seen from the road.

History

The earliest building on the site was a Roman lookout tower. Since then the coastline has retreated and the town of Hythe has grown up between Saltwood and the sea.

It is believed that Aesc, son of the Jutish warlord Hengist, built a timber fortress, with a moat, on the hill in 488 A.D. In 1026 the estate was gifted to the church by King Canute, an act of piety which would have unexpected long term consequences.

After the Norman Conquest the castle was held by the De Montfort family. The curtain wall was erected shortly after 1100 A.D., by Henry de Essex.

In the 1160s the Archbishop of Canterbury, Thomas Becket, asked King Henry II to hand the castle back to the direct control of the church. The King was not prepared to surrender control of castle with such strategic importance, and instead he appointed Sir Ranulph de Broc as castellan. This was only one small part of the spiralling conflict which was taking place between the arch-bishop and the monarch.

In June 1170 Henry had his son crowned as heir apparent at York. The ceremony was carried out by the Archbishop of York and two other bishops.

Thomas Becket was outraged that he had been bypassed, and in November of that year he excommunicated all three.

Accounts vary as to what King Henry actually said of the matter. The most common version is that the king said; "Will no one rid me of this turbulent priest."

Edward Grim, however, quoted the king as saying "What miserable drones and traitors have I nourished and brought up in my household, who let their lord be treated with such shameful contempt by a low-born cleric?"

Whatever the words used, the matter was taken up by four of Henry's knights; William de Tracey, Reginald Fitzures, Hugh de Morville and Richard le Breton. Being friends of Ranulph de Broc, they met at Saltwood Castle to plan Becket's murder. On December 29th they set off towards Canterbury, with an escort of troops provided by de Broc. After killing the Arch-Bishop they returned to Saltwood and then fled to France.

In view of the immense furore which followed Becket's death, successive kings had little choice but to leave the castle in the hands of the church.

In 1540 the castle was passed back to the crown in the course of the English Reformation. A new wing, known as the Tudor Wing, was built. It then passed to various owners but was generally uninhabited after 1580.

Saltwood Castle, detail from a work by Deeble c1818

In this image of Saltwood Castle, by Deeble, 1818, the massive gatehouse is on the right. The whole building had clearly become quite dilapidated by this time.

In the 19th and 20th centuries the castle was restored at the expense of private owners, including Lady Conway. Between 1934 and 1949 a great deal of excellent work took place and a new wing was built in the Gothic style.

Following the death of Lady Conway the castle was purchased by Sir Kenneth Clark, later Lord Clark, famous for his books and television series entitled "Civilisation." The Clark family still own the castle and have continued to restore and improve it at their own expense.

Description and Defences

In the 1160's a keep was added by Ranulph de Broc. The gatehouse is very similar in appearance to the West Gate at Canterbury. It is a solid square building fronted by two tall, cylindrical towers, which are connected by a short battlement with machicolations. There is also a portcullis and the loop holes where the chains for the drawbridge would once have passed. Directly behind the gatehouse are the Tudor Wing and the Gothic Wing, both of which have been skilfully added so that they blend in perfectly with the original medieval structure.

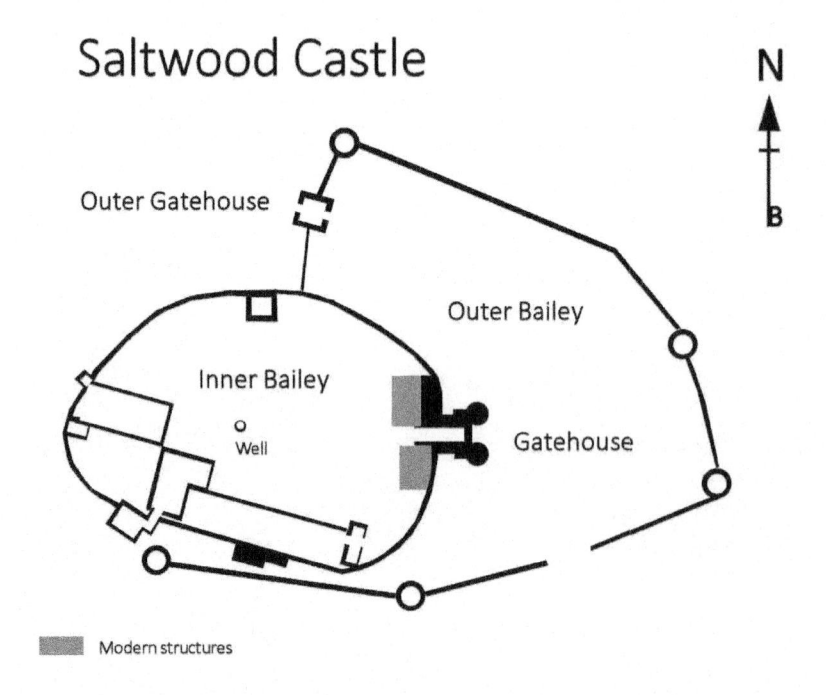

Saltwood Castle

The curtain wall around the inner bailey was erected shortly after 1100 A.D. by Henry de Essex.

It gives us an interesting example of how military architecture was evolving. The towers on the north and west side are square and situated behind the wall. By the time the southern section of the wall was built designs had evolved and the two southern towers were rounded, which made them stronger, and projected outwards, making it easier to shoot at attackers who had got in close to the bottom of the wall.

Large parts of the outer bailey walls are still standing. At the most northern point of the circuit a well preserved round tower sits near the square outer-gatehouse, which is visible from Castle Road.

Saltwood Castle, from Ireland's History of Kent, 1831

This view is from the north-west, looking across the outer gatehouse towards the north side of the main gatehouse.

The walls of the inner bailey are in good condition, with wall-walks which are still accessible.

Within the inner bailey are the remains of several half-ruined buildings, including the Knights Hall, a very romantic ruin which still has its medieval stone window tracery. There is also a well.

In the 14th century the castle was badly damaged by an earthquake, a rare event in British history. Under the direction of Archbishop Courtenay, the castle was repaired and enlarged with the creation of an outer bailey. The original castle now became the inner bailey and the old keep was rebuilt as a fine gatehouse, all around 1380.

Visiting Hythe

Whilst visiting the local area, you may wish to visit St. Leonard's Church, which is well known for its ossuary, a crypt where the bones of those buried by the church have been cleaned and stored.

Sandgate Castle

A major structure on the seafront at Sandgate. Privately owned
Postcode for Satnav: CT20 3RR
Nearest major road A259
Website: https://historicengland.org.uk/listing/the-list/list-entry/1005171
Parking Arrangements: Castle Road Car Park - CT20 3AQ
Public transport: Folkestone Central Railway Station then 16 bus towards Hythe. Disembark at Castle Road.

Also nearby
Lower Leas Coastal Park

Sandgate Castle, detail from a print by Newton, 1787

Sandgate Castle is privately owned and is closed to the public but easily visible from the road or the beach.

History

International relations, in the Tudor period, were marked by fierce rivalries between the great renaissance monarchs who ruled England, France, Austria and Spain. Matters became more ominous after 1533 due to the breakdown of relations between England and the Roman Catholic Church. By 1538 King Henry VIII was expecting an attack by France, and in response to the threat he constructed a line of coastal castles at Deal, Walmer, Sandgate and Sandown. These are sometimes described as the "Henrican Castles."

All four castles were built within two years, under the supervision of Stephan Von Haschenperg. They were designed on a geometrical plan, similar to European forts designed by Albrecht Durer, however there were certain changes to the plan as far as Sandgate was concerned.

Description and Defences

At the time it was built the castle consisted of a circular keep with 3 round towers and bastions and a gatehouse, all surrounded by 2 curtain walls, to form a triangular inner and outer ward.

Sandgate Castle

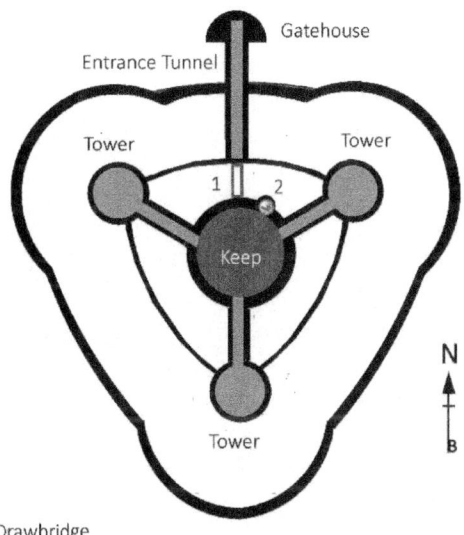

1 = Drawbridge
2 = Keep Stairwell

The overall plan is triangular, but with slightly curved walls which may have been considered to be stronger against cannon shot. The fort could bring to bear 4 tiers of artillery, and had a total of 142 firing points for cannon and handguns.

The castle was altered in the Napoleonic Wars. The walls were actually lowered, making it easier to operate artillery and making it less of a target to enemy shipping. In the eyes of most historians these alterations were badly done and have damaged a historical site, but of course, there was a war on and that took priority.

The sea has also taken its toll. About one third of the castle has been washed away by the sea, with most of the damage occurring in 1928.

Sandown Castle

A minor structure near Deal
Postcode for Satnav: CT14 6NY
Nearest major road   A256
Parking Arrangements: Sandown Road
Public transport: Deal Railway Station

Also nearby:
Deal Castle
Sandwich, historic town with medieval defences..

History

Henry VIII reigned over England from 1509 to 1547. In the 1530s he had broken away from the Roman Catholic Church and married Anne Boleyn. In 1538, fearing invasion, he began the construction of a string of coastal fortresses. Many of these have long since disappeared, either demolished or washed away by the sea.

For strategic reasons, three of the castles, at Sandown, Walmer and Deal were all built within a mile of each other, overlooking the Goodwin Sands, and were interconnected by earthwork fortifications. This part of the coast was a sheltered area for ships to anchor and it must have been seen as an obvious place for any invading force to land.

Sandown Castle was built to a concentric design, with a circular outer wall and a circular tower in the centre. Its garrison fought for Parliament in the English Civil War, but then joined the Royalists when trouble flared up again in the Second Civil War.

The only real threat came from the sea, as tidal currents gradually changed the layout of the beaches. In 1785 the sea had already broken into the moat, and by 1856 the walls were being undermined by the waves. By 1894 it had become a lost cause and the ruins were so dangerous that they were demolished by the army.

There is very little to see now, but one might suggest that by visiting Walmer Castle it is possible to see what Sandown would have been like when newly built.

Bruce W. Johnson

Sandwich Old Town with Defences and Gates

Postcode for Satnav: CT13 9EA
Nearest major road   A256
Parking Arrangements   Guildhall Car Park CT13 9AH
Public transport: Sandwich railway station

Also nearby
Fisher Gate CT13 9EN
Sandwich Barbican CT13 9EA
Sandwich Guildhall Museum CT13 9AH
Sandwich Medieval Centre CT13 9EN
US Navy P-22 Gunboat CT13 9EW
St. Bartholomew's Hospital Chapel CT13 0BP
The Dutch House, 62 King Street. CT13 9BL

Sandwich is a delightful small town, ideal for a stress-free day out. It has pretty streets, historic buildings, old pubs, quaint shops and you can easily find a nice café if you fancy a sandwich. For those seeking historic accommodation, there are no castles to lodge in but at least two historic inns. The Bell Hotel is well positioned on the quayside and the New Inn overlooks the historic market.

History
Sandwich was one of the five original cinq ports, tasked with the duty of defending the south coast against incursions by the French. This led to its importance as a fortified town. The sea has long since retreated leaving the settlement high and dry, but it still has a quayside. Historically, it also had a castle, but it fell into disuse and has long since disappeared, to be replaced by the urban defences.

It was here, at Sandwich, that King Richard the Lionheart landed back on English soil, when he returned from the crusades in 1194.

In 1217 there was a hard-fought naval battle off Sandwich, which probably deserves more attention than it has generally had. King John was involved in a bitter dispute with his own Barons, and sieges took place at both Dover and Rochester Castles. The French were supported by the Capetian Kings of France. In 1217, following the Battle of Lincoln, King John seemed to be gaining the upper hand, so the French sent a fleet of reinforcements under the command of Eustace the Monk, a colourful character, who had broken his monastic vows and had become a pirate, constantly raiding the south coast and its shipping routes. He was accompanied by one of the rebel leaders, Robert of Courtney. Their fleet was made up of around 70 ships, carrying 125 knights and a larger number of men at arms. Most of the smaller ships were carrying supplies.

On 24th August the fleets from the Cinq Ports put to sea. They got behind the French, so that they could pepper the ships with arrows. The French for their part were shooting into the wind and had little effect.

When the ships actually came together the English quickly overcame the French. Robert of Courtenay was captured and Eustace the Monk begged for his life and offered to pay a ransom of ten thousand marks of silver. The English were having none of it and Eustace was pinned down on the deck and executed with a single blow by a fellow called Stephen Crabbe. Some of the loot from the French ships was used to build the Hospital of Saint Bartholomew in Sandwich.

The outcome of this English victory was that Prince Louis of France was forced to come to terms with King John, thus ending the Barons War.

Unfortunately the town was a popular target for French attacks in the Middle-Ages. As a result it had town walls, though at first they may have been only turf banks with a wooden fence. There was also a castle, though it has long since disappeared.

In 1457 England was ruled by the feeble-minded King Henry VI and had been weakened by the wars of the Roses. The French took advantage of the situation by sending a raiding party to Kent, burning much of Sandwich to the ground. A force of around 4,000 men from Honfleur, under the command of Marshal de Breze came ashore to pillage the town, in the process murdering the mayor, John Drury. It thereafter became an established tradition, which survives to this day, that the Mayor of Sandwich wears a black robe in mourning for this ignoble deed.

Description and Defences

Dating from 1384, the Fisher Gate stands on the quay next to the drill hall. It is the only one of the original mediaeval town gates to survive and has been scheduled as an Ancient Monument Grade I listed building.

The 14th century Barbican stands at the top of the High Street, numbers 1 - to 4. For many years it served as a toll house, charging traffic to use the bridge over the River Stour.

After the sacking of the town in 1457 an improved wall was built around the town creating a structure known as the Great Bulwark. If you start from the Sandwich Medieval Centre and walk east, with the river on your left, then the bulwark is on your right until you reach the tennis club.

A recent discovery

In 2014 a new page was, quite literally, added to the history of Sandwich, when Kent archivist Dr Mark Bateson was researching a copy of "The

Charter of the Forest," which had once been granted to Sandwich. In the archives of Kent County Council he came across a Victorian scrap book which, to his amazement, contained an original copy of the Magna Carta. Although damaged with about one third missing, it was estimated to be worth as much as £10 million, partly because it was found together with "The Charter of the Forest." As many as fifty copies of Magna Carta were written. Of those, only 24 still exist, but this is only the second one to still be accompanied by the Charter of the Forest.

Scotney Castle

A major structure near Tonbridge Wells. National Trust.
Postcode for Satnav: TN3 8JN - but please read the warning at the bottom of this entry.
Nearest major road   A21
Website: https://www.nationaltrust.org.uk/visit/kent/scotney-castle
Parking Arrangements: Pay parking on site

Also nearby
Bayham Old Abbey

Scotney Castle is famed for its gardens, which are officially listed as a site of special scientific interest. The location is open to the public and is popular with visiting tourists.

If you are genuinely looking for medieval castles then there is not a great deal to see as there is little left of the old castle, just one very romantic tower overlooking a beautiful lake. However the ruin is remarkably atmospheric and provides almost the perfect background for a photograph.

The new house, built by Hussey is also open to visitors, but it is a minor stately home from the Victorian era, a little too new for my tastes and definitely not a castle in the traditional sense.

On the other hand, the gardens planned by Edward Hussey in the Victorian era are now fully mature and quite spectacular. If you actually enjoy walking round extensive beautiful gardens you can have an extremely pleasant day at Scotney, and if you are already a member of the National Trust then your day out will cost considerably less.

Description and Defences
The original castle had stone walls topped with timber framed accommodation, and four circular stone towers, one at each corner, all surrounded by a moat. Entry to the main castle was via a barbican, perched on a stone island. Both the castle and the barbican had drawbridges.

History
Scotney Castle is named after its first known owner, Sir Lambert di Scoteni, who owed fealty to the Lords of Leeds Castle in 1237. The actual name may be connected to a place in France, called Escotigny close to Foucarmont in the region of the Seine Inferieur. There is no connetion to Scotland.

Scotney Castle

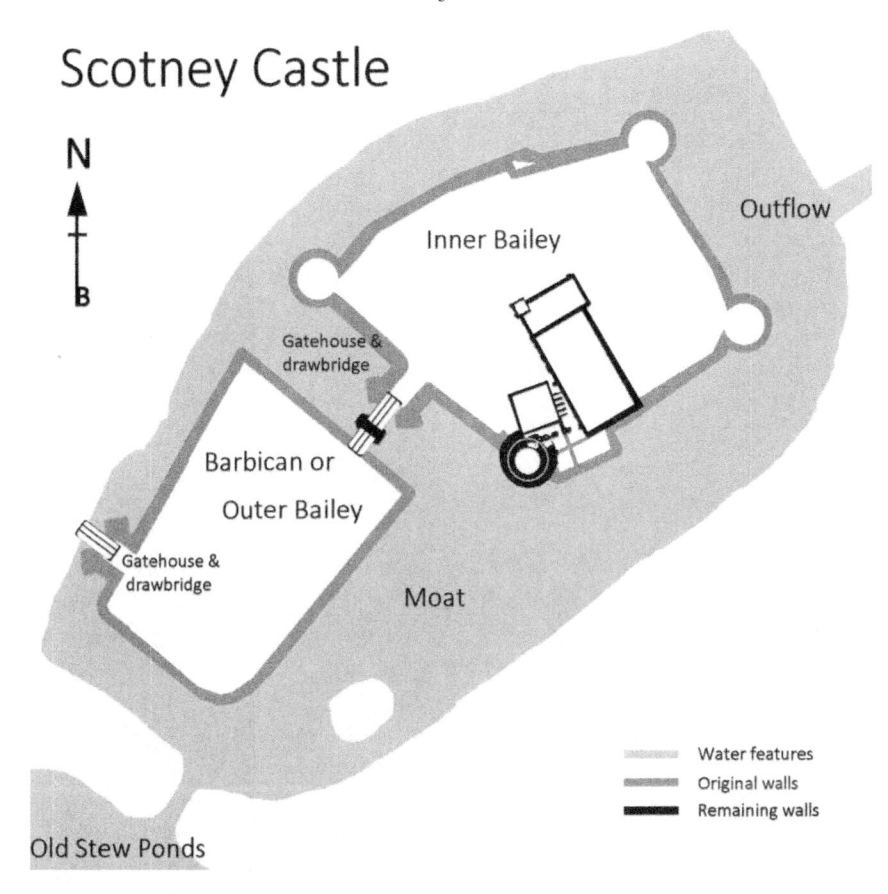

N ↑

- Outflow
- Inner Bailey
- Gatehouse & drawbridge
- Barbican or Outer Bailey
- Gatehouse & drawbridge
- Moat
- Water features
- Original walls
- Remaining walls

Old Stew Ponds

Walter de Scoteni was hanged at Winchester in 1259 for poisoning William de Clare, though it seems that he may have been innocent. This was the period of the Baron's Wars, and a year earlier the Barons had managed to have court orders granted against the King's half-brothers, the Valence family, forcing them into exile.

Before they left, William de Valence, Bishop of Winchester, organised a banquet but several of the guests took ill with symptoms of poisoning. William de Clare died and William de Valence, Earl of Pembroke, suffered a long illness with terrible symptoms including the loss of his hair and teeth. Walter de Scoteni was put on trial and the case against him was that William de Valence had paid him to poison William de Clare in order to get revenge for being sent into exile. This clearly makes no sense as William de Valence was also poisoned.

After the Barons Wars Scotney Castle was taken into the ownership of the crown.

Castles of Kent

The present castle was built by Sir Roger Ashburnham between 1378 and 1380, in response to ongoing French attacks on the south coast. There are doubts as to whether the full structure was ever properly completed and as early as 1558 it seems to have fallen into disrepair with only one tower still standing but the building was still in use as a residence.

Between 1591 and 1598 the owner was Thomas Darrel, was a recusant, a secret Roman Catholic at a time when the official religion was Protestantism.

It is said that in 1598 a Roman Catholic priest known as Father Blount was given refuge in the castle when it was raided by three magistrates with troops intent on capturing him. The priest and his servant, a man called Bray, managed to hide in a secret chamber, known as a priest's hole. They had hardly any clothing and nothing to eat or drink apart from one loaf and a bottle of wine.

The family were sent away and the authorities searched the buildings for ten days, with the help of masons and carpenters looking for the secret passages.

Eventually Blount decided that he had to escape. He climbed up into one of the towers at night and leapt down 16 feet into the moat which was so cold it had a thin covering of ice. After swimming 80 feet he managed to crawl to the house of a servant who was also a catholic, and subsequently escaped to safety.

In the civil war period much of the house was rebuilt by William Darrel. It remained in the hands of the Darrels for around 350 years though the family had mixed fortunes during that time.

In 1836 the owner, Edward Hussey, decided to build a new house at the top of the hill, overlooking the ruin. Many aristocrats of the period paid to have Gothic follies built for decorative purposes. Hussey had his romantic ruin already in place and simply had his landscaped gardens built around it. Unusually, especially in Kent, the estate had its own source of high quality building stone. In effect the new castle was built from sandstone quarried straight from the slope below. The hollow space which this created was developed into a Quarry Garden and contains a 100-million-year-old impression of a dinosaur's footprint.

Hussey also constructed an "Ice House" in the grounds, for cold storage in the years before refrigerators.

After 1970 the House was left to the National Trust. Several apartments on the estate were let out and one of the new residents was Mrs. Margaret Thatcher, the Prime Minister. So attached were the Thatchers to their weekend retreat that Mr. Dennis Thatcher later took the title "Baronet Thatcher of Scotney in the County of Kent."

At the time of writing [2022] Scotney Castle and Gardens are available as a high quality wedding venue, for further information see the National Trust website; https://www.nationaltrust.org.uk/venue-hire

Travel Warning:

The road which was once the entrance to the estate is now the exit. Some Sat-Navs will direct you to this exit which opens directly off the roundabout. I advise you to ignore your Satnav when you reach the roundabout and follow the brown road signs which will direct you onto the B2169 where you will find the castle entrance on your right.

Severndroog Castle

A major structure near Shooters Hill, London.
Owned by the Severndroog Castle Building Preservation Trust 2003
Postcode for Satnav: SE18 3RT
Nearest major road   A205 / A207
Website: https://www.severndroogcastle.org.uk/
Public transport: Falconwood or Eltham stations
Parking Arrangements: Some parking spaces on the approach road, and a parking lot 2 streets to the east, but check for signs and charges.

Also nearby
Park Wood [Ancient dedicious forest]
Oxleas Wood [Ancient dedicious forest]
Shrewsbury Tumulus [Bronze Age burial mound]
Eltham Palace.
Greenwich Park and Historic Buildings
Well Hall Pleasaunce; Park with Tudor barn housing art gallery.

History

Severndroog Castle is a Gothic style "Folly" built in 1784 by Lady James, as a memorial to her husband. It is now owned by a trust who have restored the building. It is open to the public and is used as a centre for community activities. It is an ideal spot for families who live in London and want to go somewhere different for a day out. Please check the website for exact details and opening times.

At the time of writing [2022] Severndroog is available as a venue for weddings. See the website for further details, under venue hire.

Bruce W. Johnson

Severndroog Tower, detail, by Edward Wedlake Brayley c1815

Shoreham Castle

A minor redeveloped site near Orpington, Privately owned
Postcode for Satnav: TN14 7UD
Nearest major road M20 / A225

Also nearby
Shoreham Aircraft Museum
Lullingstone Castle and World Farm
Lullingstone Roman Villa
Eynsford Castle

History
Castle Farm stands on Castle Road in a bend of the River Darent. There was once a small castle at this location, owned by the church but held by a succession of Kent families with names like Osborne Peyforer, Hugo de Poyntz and Sir Roger de Chaundois. By the Tudor period it had passed from the Newborough family to the Polhills, whose name is preserved in the nearby Polhill farm, but by then the actual building was already in ruins.

Information for visitors
There is nothing significant to see here and I would not advise making a visit, but it is interesting to know what once was as you travel towards some of the other attractions in the area.

Bruce W. Johnson

Shurland Hall

A major structure near Eastchurch. Privately owned
Postcode for Satnav: ME12 4BN
Nearest major road A2500
Website: https://www.thespitalfieldstrust.com/project/new-shurland-hall-eastchurch-isle-of-sheppey-kent/
Parking Arrangements - roadside.
Public transport: Nothing close.

Also nearby
Eastchurch Aviation Museum

Located out on the north east corner of Eastchurch just past the cricket club, Shurland Castle, or Shurland Hall, is actually the gatehouse of what was once a most impressive Tudor palace, on the Isle of Sheppey. It has been connected with two of Sheppey's most famous families from the Middle-Ages, the de Shurlands and the Cheyneys. In modern times it has become an example of how an ancient building can be rescued from the ravages of time and restored to at least some of its former glory.

Shurland Hall

Design and Appearance
The original Shurland Hall was a Norman castle, occupied by the de Shurland family for many years. It passed by inheritance to Sir Thomas Cheyne in 1496. Apparently he did not like the old defensive structure and

so between 1510 and 1518 he oversaw the construction of a splendid new hall, surrounded by a complex of walled quadrangles.

Built at a time when England was internally peaceful, this was not a defensive site, but rather a "stately residence" no expense spared in its construction. It is believed that stone from the old castle was reused in the construction but that simply wasn't enough and Sheppey has no quarries yielding high quality building stone so the bulk of the material for the walls around the gardens had to be brought to the island, much of it having been robbed from Chilham Castle which Thomas Cheyne also owned. Shurland served as the main hall to a huge estate that took in most farms and marshes on the eastern end of Sheppey. The gatehouse, as we see it today, is constructed in the stylish redbrick of the period and it features the octagonal towers and high chimney stacks which are so characteristic of other Tudor palaces such as Hampton Court.

Shurland Hall

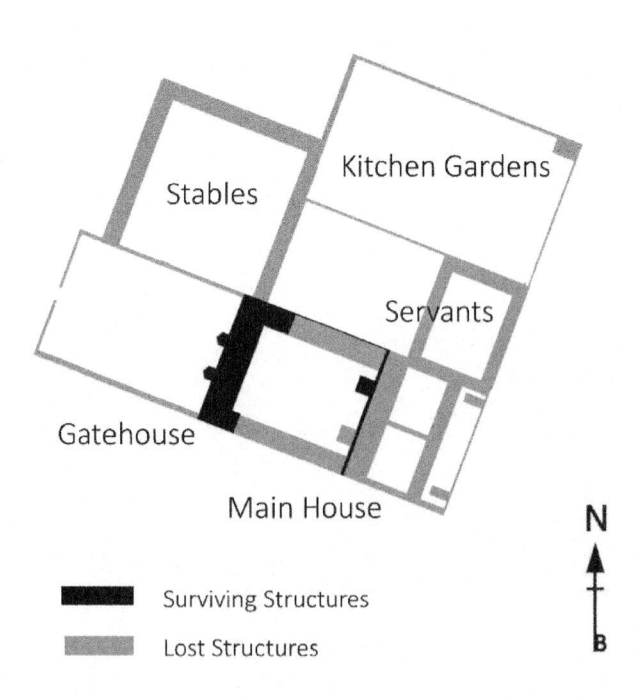

The site includes seven acres of grounds including a lake, substantial 16th-century stone and brick garden walls and the stone remains of the medieval great hall itself.

Bruce W. Johnson

History

Thomas Cheyney had served as squire to Henry the VIII and he shared a love of jousting with the King. Consequently he rose rapidly in Henry's favour. He became Sheriff of Kent and Lord of the Cinque Ports and ended up as a Privy Councillor. For a time he was the most powerful man in Kent, especially after he was given former church land on the Isle of Sheppey and North Kent.

In 1532 King Henry VIII and his new wife Anne Boleyn stayed at the Hall for a few days whilst en-route to see Francis I in France. They were entertained at immense financial expense by Sir Thomas Cheyne, with great feasts and much hunting on the estate.

Henry Cheyney, son of Thomas, chose to dispose of his father's Kent property, in favour of his mother's estate in Bedfordshire, and this marked the beginning of the rather rapid decline of Shurland Hall.

In the First World War the building was used as a military base, leading to much damage. It was used again in World War Two but after that it was largely unoccupied and by the 1980s it had fallen into a state of ruin, with a roof which leaked badly causing further damage to the rest of the property.

Fortunately it was acquired by the Spitalfields Trust in 2006 and underwent a major programme of restoration, both inside and out. This included replacing the Hall's derelict roof, rebuilding the chimneys, re-pointing large parts of the outside and repairing all the inside rooms, including tasteful repair and replacement of wooden staircases. These works were carried out to very high standards in order to preserve the historical validity of the building. One particular example is that the Tudor chimneys had to be rebuilt exactly as they were, using old photographs as a guide and even using mortar mixed with ground up fragments of seashells, as was the case in the original building. One has to give credit to the modern day female bricklayer who carried out the work.

Since 2013 Shurland has been occupied as a private dwelling and was placed on the market for £2.5 Million in 2018.

Media Information

Shurland is a private residence and not open to the public, although it can be seen from the road. Some internal photographs may be seen on line;

https://www.kentlive.news/news/kent-news/gallery/full-look-around-sheerness-shurland-2323119

https://www.thespitalfieldstrust.com/project/new-shurland-hall-eastchurch-isle-of-sheppey-kent/

Sissinghurst Castle & Gardens

A major site near Ashford. National Trust
Postcode for Satnav: TN17 2AB
Nearest major road   M20 / A21
Website: https://www.nationaltrust.org.uk/sissinghurst-castle-garden
Parking Arrangements: Carpark on site for visitors

Also nearby
Cranbrook Common
Staplehurst Village
Sutton Valence Castle

For those who enjoy strolling through beautiful gardens I would recommend Sissinghurst at almost any time of the year as long as the weather is to your taste.

Sissinghurst, detail from Allen's History of Cranbrook c1700

History
Originally known as Saxingherste, the manor house on this site dates back to at least the 12th century. It was sold to Thomas Baker in 1490 and rebuilt as a Tudor red-brick mansion. His son Richard Baker then demolished it again, around 1560, and replaced it with another grand house in the Elizabethan style. Queen Elizabeth I actually stayed in the house for three days in 1573.

Subsequently the house fell into disrepair and was even used as a prison for French soldiers and sailors during the Seven Years War, between 1756 and 1763. Angered by their poor food and squalid conditions, the prisoners of war caused a great deal of damage to the property. By 1800 most of the building had to be pulled down.

Fortunately, in the 1930s, the property was rescued by Victoria Sackville-West, who began the restoration of what remained and set out to create the magnificent landscaped gardens which are visited by large numbers of tourists every year.

Sissinghurst, the Tudor Gatehouse

Description and Defences
Sissinghurst was built as a palatial stately home, and was never really a castle in the military sense, but there remains an impressive gatehouse, from the Tudor period, built of red brick with octagonal flanking towers.

At the time of writing [2022] it was possible to hire Sissinghurst as a high quality wedding venue. For details see the National Trust website and look under venue hire.

Starkey Castle

A minor structure near Rochester
Postcode for Satnav: ME1 3TR
Nearest major road   A228
Privately owned

Also nearby
Rochester Castle and Cathedral
Gundulph's Tower
Rochester High Street and Museum

History
 The village of Wouldham historically had three manors. The overlord of all three was the Bishop of Rochester. One of the subordinate manors was called Littlehall and the other enjoyed the unusual title of "The Manor of the Rings."
 Humphrey Starkey had been the Recorder of London since 1473 and was a supporter of King Richard III who rewarded him with a knighthood in 1483. Two years later, when King Henry VII seized the crown he appointed Sir Humphrey to the post of Chief Baron of the Exchequer. Considering how careful Henry was in financial matters, this suggests that Starkey was a seen as a competent and trustworthy man.
 In 1490 Sir Humphrey Starkey bought the Littlehall Estate. It is not clear whether the actual manor house was built at that time, or earlier by Richard Byset in 1390.

Description
 Starkey's Castle can be described as a double-solar hall house. It consists of a hall and a tower. It is now a grade 1 listed historic building and is considere to be one of the best surviving examples of a stone-built medieval hall-house. The original timbers supporting the main roof are still in excellent condition. The castle is just a short walk upriver from Rochester Castle. There have always been rumours of underground tunnels linking the Manor House to Wouldham Church, Cuxton Church, and the main castle, however there seems little reason for such extensive tunnelling and no remains have ever been found.
 It is not possible to explore the building as it is now a private home, but it may be glimpsed on the left when travelling north up Wouldham High Street.

Bruce W. Johnson

Stockbury Castle

A minor site near Gillingham. Privately owned
Postcode for Satnav: ME9 7RD
Nearest major road   M2 / A 249

History

It appears that the Stockbury site was originally a prehistoric camp, protected by earthworks. A castle was built just after the Norman Conquest and was held by the Auberville family from 1082. Later it passed to Sir Nicholas de Kiriel [or Criol] and his family held it until 1460.

The site then fell into ruin, and the land was used for farming. The farmhouse was not part of the castle, but was built in the 17th Century.

Description

Originally there was a wall made from flint and mortar surrounded by a ditch, and then a larger, semi-circular, bailey yard. However at some point half of the defences were levelled and a church was built. No recognisable structures have survived, only ditches which mark the prehistoric defences and a slight hump which was the medieval mote. Only one small section of the walls now remain.

Stone Castle

A major structure near Dartford.
Privately owned, not open to the public.

Postcode for Satnav: DA9 9XL [See below for further details]
Nearest major road   A2
Parking Arrangements - on street.

History
Stone Castle stood on land owned by the church and controlled by the Bishops of Rochester. Sir John Northwood held it in the reign of Edward III. In the time of Henry VIII it was held by Sir John Wyllshire.

All that now remains of Stone Castle is a square medieval tower, which has been incorporated into a mock Gothic Building of the Victorian Era. To be fair, the Victorian building is in itself quite pleasing to the eye and blends in well with the original tower, which is the section on the left of this picture.

Stone Castle, Kent.

Travel Information for visitors
As you approach the general area of the castle you will probably reach a large roundabout where the A206 meets the A226 London Road, close to St Mary's Church. With the church behind you follow London Road for a very short distance and you may see a small green sign pointing the way to Stone Castle. Turn into Sanderling Way, which then becomes Stone Castle Drive.

There is a sign on the gate stating that it is private property, however you may not see it as the gate is often left standing open. In any case the tower can easily be seen and photographed from the road.

Stutfall Castle

A minor site near Hythe
Postcode for Satnav: CT21 4LQ
Nearest major road   M20 / A 259
On Private land but close to a footpath.

Also nearby
Lympne Castle and village
Port Lympne Safari Park
West Hythe Dam
Ruins of St. Mary's Church

History
   The village of Lympne takes its name from the Roman fort known as "Portus Lemanis." The original fort seems to have collapsed, perhaps due to underground water eroding the chalk and clay upon which it was built. All that remains are some tumbled walls.
   In its prime it was a large establishment, around 200 meters by 250 Meters, the equivalent of five football fields. The walls, mainly built from flint and cement, would have been around 25 feet high, and almost certainly arranged in the "playing card shape" which was standard for military encampments across the Roman Empire.
   There is little to see of the fort itself, but the site provides for an excellent view of Lympne Castle, perched on the hillside above.

Sutton Valence Castle

A minor site near Maidstone
Postcode for Satnav: ME17 3BS [See note below]
Nearest major road   M20
Website:
English Heritage
Parking Arrangements
Public transport:

Also nearby
Leeds Castle
Buttercups Sanctuary for Goats. ME17 4JW

Sutton Valence is a beautiful small town in the heart of rural Kent. With its picturesque buildings and quaint old pubs, it is worth visiting for its own sake. At the time of writing [2022] the official website gives the postcode of the castle as ME17 3LW but this is not correct and will land you in another part of the town. Use ME17 3BS, which will take you along a very narrow road called Rectory Lane.

If you are using a satnav device, it may take you past the castle, so you need to stop when you see it. It is hard to miss, towering over the road, and the steps leading up to it are steep and uneven, so tread carefully.

History

There is much we do not know regarding Sutton Valence Castle. It has been suggested that Baldwin de Bethune, the Norman count of Aumale, probably built the castle in the middle of the 12th century.

Later the demesne passed to William le Gros, Earl of Albermarle, around 1200, and was then passed on to the Mareschal family who were Earls of Pembroke. Later it was owned by Eleanor, the daughter of King John, but around 1238 it passed, by marriage, to his political opponent Simon de Montfort, sixth Earl of Leicester.

Simon was the leader of the baronial rebellion against King Henry III. He was killed at the Battle of Evesham in 1265, and his estates were confiscated by the Crown. The king then granted it to his half-brother, William de Valence as a reward for his support during the rebellion. The village of Sutton, or 'south town', became known as Sutton Valence. William's son, Aymer de Valence, inherited the castle in 1307. After this date, very little is known about the history of the castle. This site is now in the care of English Heritage.

Bruce W. Johnson

Sutton Valence Castle

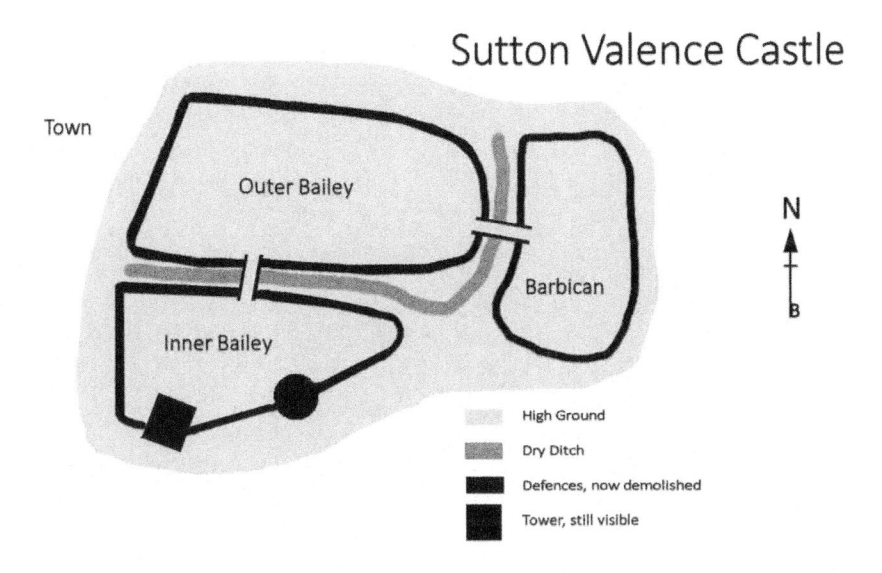

Map legend:
- High Ground
- Dry Ditch
- Defences, now demolished
- Tower, still visible

Labels on map: Town, Outer Bailey, Inner Bailey, Barbican, N

Description and Defences

Sutton Valence castle was situated in a strong position, dominating the Weald of Kent. Perhaps of greater importance, the town sits astride the road from Rye, leading north towards Maidstone. This gave the castle considerable strategic importance. If an army had landed at Dover their route would have been blocked by the castles at Dover, Canterbury and Rochester. To avoid these hazards an invading army could have landed at Winchelsea and marched on London from there. Sutton Valence Castle was ideally placed to prevent such an attack.

Little now remains of the castle other than the lower section of a small square keep, 12 meters square, with walls around 2.5 meters thick. The ruins reach a height of 9 meters but would originally have been much higher, perhaps three storeys reaching as much as 20 meters. As with many such buildings, the entrance is at first floor level which made it difficult for attackers to use battering rams.

There was also a round tower and some sections of wall which have since disappeared.

When the castle fell into disrepair the grounds it once occupied were given over to farming. The remaining fragments seem rather sad, dilapidated and broken. This melancholy effect is perhaps a result of the poor quality of the remaining stonework, small flints and other rubble held together with crumbling mortar. In fact, the apparent shortage of good building stone does beg the question as to whether the outer walls were ever built in stone, or remained just timber palisades. Hopefully some future excavation will shed light on this.

Castles of Kent

Sutton Valence Castle: The Great Tower

Thurnham Castle

A minor structure near Maidstone owned by Kent County Council.
Postcode for Satnav: ME14 3LE
Nearest major road   M20 A249
Parking Arrangements: roadside.
Public transport:

Also nearby
White Horse Country Park.
Aylesford Village
Leeds Castle

History
　　The site of Thurnham appears to have been a prehistoric camp and significant earthwork ditches can still be seen. These would have helped the Normans who constructed a steep motte and bailey castle built shortly after the Norman Conquest on land granted to Bishop Odo. The stone Castle followed and was later passed to Robert Corbye of Broughton Malherbe. A few broken pieces of the stone walls can still be seen although from old accounts it seems that much of it was destroyed in the 20th Century, when people ought to have known better.
　　During the Second World War the hilltop was used as a lookout post by members of the Royal Observer Corps, part-time volunteers who would watch for enemy aircraft coming over the channel and would telephone warnings through to the RAF fighter command centre. The motto on their badge was "Forewarned is Forearmed" which is a popular English proverb.

Tonbridge Castle

A major structure owned by Tonbridge and Malling Borough Council
Postcode for Satnav: TN9 1BG
Nearest major road   A26
Website: https://www.tonbridgecastle.org/
Parking Arrangements: Lower Castle Field Car Park, TN9 1HR
Public transport: Tonbridge Railway Station

Also nearby
Chiddingstone Village
Penshurst Place

History

Following the Norman Conquest, the Tonbridge demesne was granted to Richard FitzGilbert who erected a wooden castle with two baileys. His grandson, Richard Fitz Gilbert, died in battle in Wales and in 1152 the castle passed to Roger, Earl of Hereford and Clare.

For over a century there was an ongoing dispute over the management of the castle. The church claimed to own it, but the various kings continued to choose the castellan from among their supporters. At one point the Pope excommunicated everyone living in the castle.

Gilbert de Clare was one of the rebellious barons who forced King John to sign the Magna Carta in 1215. In revenge, King John besieged and captured Tonbridge Castle.

The de Clare family line died out in 1314 when the last Gilbert de Clare was killed at the Battle of Bannockburn in Scotland. The castle then passed by the female line to the king's favourite, Hugh Despencer. When he was executed the castle passed to Hugh de Audley and then to his daughter Margaret who married Lord Stafford. Tonbridge Castle then stayed with the Staffords until 1520 when Edmund Stafford was executed by King Henry VIII.

The castle was not lived in between 1521 and the late 18th century, except for a short period during the English Civil War, when it was held by a parliamentary supporter Mr. Thomas Weller, and managed to hold out against a royalist attack in 1643.

The mansion was added in 1793. In Victorian times the castle was used as a school, and in 1860 as a military academy.

In 1897 the local authority decided to purchase the castle as part of the celebrations for Queen Victoria's Diamond Jubilee.

In 1900, the entire site was purchased by the local council, who now use the mansion as offices, and who made the grounds a public park. Both castle and mansion are Grade I listed buildings.

The castle is also the start of a 6-mile cycle ride to Penshurst Place, known as the Tudor Trail.

Tonbridge Castle by Baines c1829.

Description and Defences

At the time it was built, Tonbridge Castle would have been a text-book example of what we call a Motte and Bailey Castle.

The "Motte" is the large mound of earth on which the keep stood. It is over 20 meters high and the flat area on top is 77 meters wide. The "Bailey" is the castle yard. Tonbridge had two baileys, the inner bailey, to the south east of the motte and the outer bailey to the north-west. At first the keep and the fences would have been made from timber, but later rebuilt in stone. The keep was oval shaped, had two entrances, and was lined with timber buildings within. The castle also had a moat which was fed from the river Medway.

The great gatehouse at Tonbridge is one of the most impressive features of the site. It was constructed around 1270. It was very well defended with a portcullis for every outward facing doorway. The main hall of the gatehouse was impressive in itself.

There was also, at one time, a water-gate or water-tower, where passengers from boats could enter the castle, but that has completely disappeared.

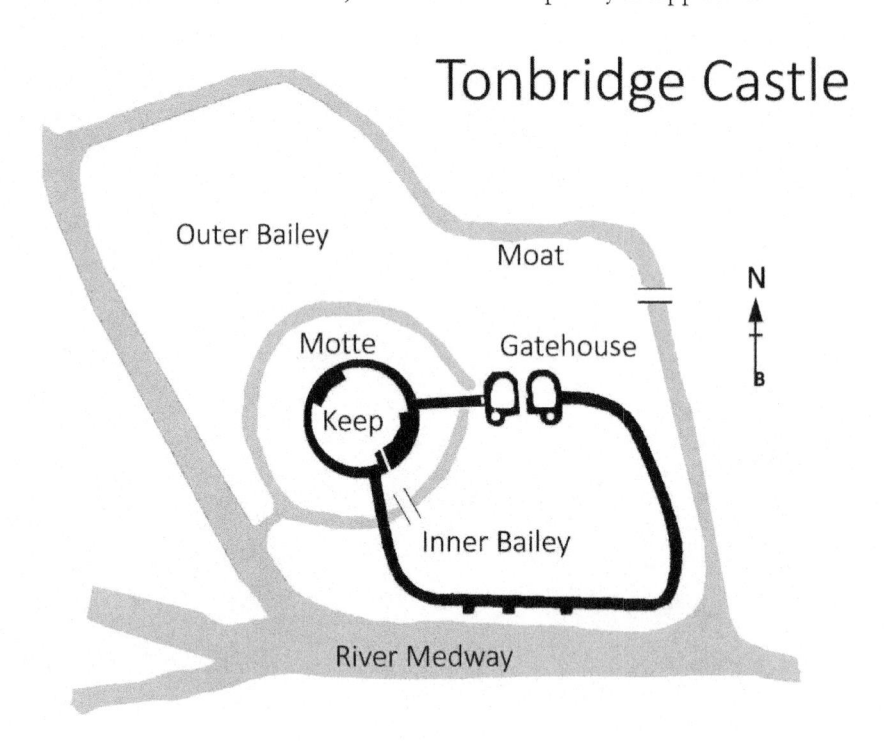

Tonbridge Castle

Outer Bailey
Moat
N
Motte
Gatehouse
Keep
Inner Bailey
River Medway

Bruce W. Johnson

Upnor Castle

A major structure near Rochester; English Heritage
Postcode for Satnav: ME2 4XG
Nearest major road   A2
Website: https://www.english-heritage.org.uk/visit/places/upnor-castle/

Parking Arrangements:
Do NOT try to drive all the way to the castle. It stands at the bottom of a very narrow historic street with nowhere to park and little room for turning round.
There is a small car park on the other side of Upchat Road, ME24UP.
There is also a larger public car park in Lower Upnor, ME2 4XB
On street parking is sometimes possible in Admiralty Lane.

Also nearby:
Upnor Village
Rochester Castle
Chatham Naval Dockyard
Temple Manor, Strood ME2 2AH

On my very first evening in Kent two friends took me out to a pretty little village with a friendly pub. That village was Upnor and it remains to this day a lovely place to visit, but remarkably small, even by small village standards. With that in mind, do not attempt to get all the way to the fort by car, you are liable to get stuck in a very narrow street with no parking allowed.

History
Upnor Castle is situated on the River Medway, directly opposite the site of the Royal Navy Dockyard, Chatham, which is an appropriate indication of how closely connected the two have always been.

Henry VIII had a passion for the navy. He expanded it. He loved to inspect it. Most of all, he relied on it to fend off the risk of French invasion. London had docks but they were not suitable for the military fleet which needed to be able to get to sea quickly in an emergency. Henry thus needed a large, sheltered inlet right on the coast. The River Medway met his requirements perfectly. He bought a sizeable parcel of land on the north side of Gillingham and began to create a dockyard. By the time Queen Elizabeth I came to the throne in 1558, the Chatham Dockyard had become so important that the Queen had a defensive building erected on the opposite side of the Medway to protect against seaborne raiders. The castle was begun in 1559 under the direction of Sir Richard Lee and took 5 years to complete.

Lee's design called for a stone keep defended by a pointed bastion jutting out into the river. In 1599 the original castle was enlarged with a curtain wall on the landward side, defended by a ditch. Within the ditch was a large gatehouse, and a pair of towers were added, one on either side of the stone keep.

Sadly, when a Dutch fleet under Admiral de Ruyter attacked the Medway in 1667 the artillery at Upnor failed to stop them.

The Dutch warships exchanged fire with batteries at Upnor Castle and managed to burn three English warships before withdrawing and leaving the navigational channel partially blocked with half-sunk ships. The Dutch had suffered heavy casualties, but Upnor Castle had failed in its mission to protect the dockyard. There were three design factors which contributed to this;

The cannon positioned inside the fort had to fire out through gun ports which gave them a very narrow field of fire. They could shoot straight out across the Medway but could not hit anything upriver or down river.

The outdoor platform was V shaped, with half of the cannons facing up-river and the others down-river. This meant that whether the enemy were approaching or retreating, only half of those guns could be used at any one time.

There are also bends in the river so that by the time the enemy ships came into view they were already very close to the castle, perhaps only 600 meters. They were therefore able to sail past the castle more quickly than the guns could be manoeuvred and reloaded to aim at them.

As a result of this rather disappointing performance, new defences had to be constructed elsewhere. The castle remained with the military authorities, though mainly used for training and for storage. In 1961 it was transferred to the Ministry of Works and is now owned by English Heritage but operated by Rochester Council.

The Royal Naval Dockyard, which it was intended to protect, continued to operate throughout the two world wars and had performed one final act for the nation in 1982, when ships from Chatham set out as part of the British Task Force which liberated the Falkland Islands. The dockyard was then closed as an economy measure and it is now a museum and cultural centre. Upnor castle still watches over it.

Description and Defences

Upnor Castle is particularly distinguished by two features; a triangular bastion jutting out into the river, and low firing platforms intended to house artillery which could strike enemy ships close to the water line. The bastion is protected by a timber palisade which projects even further out into the water, possibly to prevent enemy troops, or local thieves, from getting access to the firing platforms.

Bruce W. Johnson

Upnor Castle as viewed across the River Medway.

Note that the main firing platform is the low crenelated structure just visible above the wooden fence.

Behind the bastion the main structure of the castle follows a more traditional model with a keep and high towers, capable of resisting an infantry attack from the landward side. There was also an outer ditch around the entire property, another precaution against land based attack, but all of this was intended to ensure that the guns pointing out across the water should not be silenced. It was intended that in the event of a major attack the castle garrison would hold back enemy troops while the cannons on the bastion continued to shoot at enemy ships.

When I last visited Upnor I was able to park my car in "Admiralty Lane." This street was previously known as "Powder Monkey Lane." In years gone by it was unsafe to have sacks of gunpowder close to the actual cannons which were firing on board ship. The "Powder Monkeys" were the young boys who ran back and forth carrying the bags of gunpowder from the powder store to the cannons. The name of the street was recently changed to Admiralty Lane as it was considered politically unacceptable to use the term "Powder Monkey."

At the time of writing [2022] it was possible to book Upnor Castle for wedding ceremonies. Arrangements are made through Medway Council; Email: upnor . castle @ medway . gov . uk or Telephone: 01634 718 742

Vanbrugh House

A privately owned house in Greenwich, London.
Postcode for Satnav: SE10 8XQ
Nearest major road   A2

Also nearby;
Greenwich Park.
Royal Observatory and meridian line
Cutty Sark, the National Maritime Museum,
Old Royal Naval College including the famous Painted Hall.
London's cable car,
Greenwich Market,
The O2 Arena.

Vanbrugh Castle is the name given to a Baroque-Gothic style house on Maze Hill, close to Greenwich Park. It was designed and commissioned by Sir John Vanbrugh as his own family residence.

Completed in 1719, it cannot really be classed as a castle, but it does stand as a very good illustration of that fascination with the past which marked the Enlightenment, the Romantic Movement and the Victorian era.

Bruce W. Johnson

Walmer Castle

A major site in Walmer: English Heritage
Postcode for Satnav: CT14 7LJ
Nearest major road   A256 / Kingsdown Road.
Website: https://www.english-heritage.org.uk/visit/places/walmer-castle-and-gardens/
Parking Arrangements: Kingsdown Car Park, 200 meters north of Castle CT14 7LH

Also nearby
Old Walmer Court CT14 7RP. The original Walmer Castle, from medieval times, now a ruin, visible from the church yard.

History
By 1538 King Henry VIII had broken away from the Roman Catholic Church and was expecting an attack by France. In response to the threat he constructed a line of coastal castles at Deal, Walmer, Sandgate and Sandown.

All four castles were built within two years, and were designed on a geometrical plan, similar to European forts designed by Albrecht Durer.

By deliberate design, three of the castles, at Sandown, Walmer and Deal were all built within a mile of each other, overlooking the Goodwin Sands, and were interconnected by earthwork fortifications. This part of the coast was a sheltered area for ships to anchor and it must have been seen as an obvious place for an invading force to land.

In reality the French did not invade and the castle saw no real action until the Second Civil War of 1648, when the garrison declared for the King but were forced to surrender after a short siege.

In 1708 Walmer was adapted to serve as the official residence of the Warden of the Cinq Ports, nowadays something of an honorary title. It was very popular with the Duke of Wellington who seems to have made it his home from home during the later years of his life. He actually died at Walmer in 1852.

Description and Defences
The outer defence of Walmer Castle is a very deep, steep dry moat. The entire castle sits inside this, so that most of the outer walls are beneath ground level and therefore well protected from the artillery fire of enemy ships standing off at sea. The main defences consist of four circular bastions and in the centre there is a keep which serves as a watchtower as well as providing an internal connection between all of the floors. Within the defences, the

castle is very atmospheric, with underground passageways snaking right round the bottom of the outer defences. The walls are well provided with embrasures, small holes suitable for shooting out of, and the largest guns would have been up on top of the bastions.

Walmer Castle

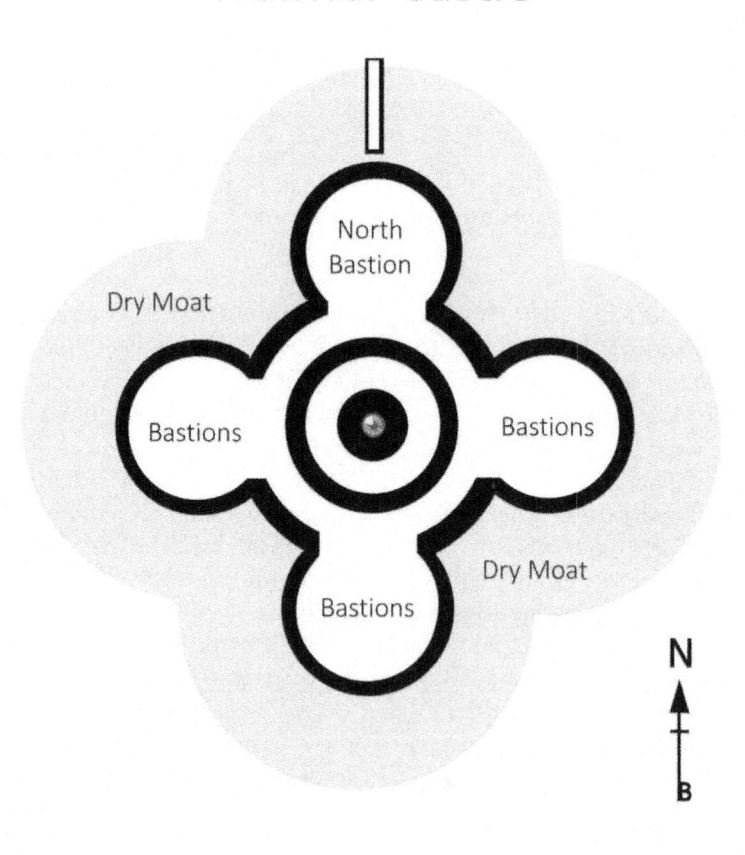

Bruce W. Johnson

Walmer: Old Walmer Court

A minor structure in Walmer. Privately owned - no entry to the public, but can be seen from the church grounds.
Postcode for Satnav: CT14 7RP
Nearest major road   A258. Website: http://www.walmerweb.co.uk/old-walmer-court.html
Parking Arrangements: on street
Public transport:

Also nearby
Church: Blessed St Mary of Walmer
Walmer Castle

Not to be confused with Walmer Castle, Old Walmer Court is the remains of a semi-fortified manor house which now sits tucked away among the side streets of the town. It is actually on private land, but you can get quite a good view of the building from the grave-yard of the Church next door.

History
Old Walmer Court may have been built for Sir William d'Auberville in the 12th century.

Description and Defences
The house was roughly square, with turrets on the corners of the walls, and an external staircase leading to the entrance door on the first floor. Obviously this was a defensive feature; it is much harder to break down a door when standing at the top of a staircase, because it isn't so easy to use a battering ram.

Originally there was a moat which encircled and protected both the manor house and the Blessed Mary of Walmer Church.

West Malling: Saint Leonards Tower

A minor structure near Maidstone, English Heritage
Postcode for Satnav: ME19 6PD
Nearest major road M20
Website: https://www.english-heritage.org.uk/visit/places/st-leonards-tower/
Parking Arrangements:
Manor Park Country Park, opposite the tower has a car park at ME19 6PE, however, I found it possible to park on the roadside.
Public transport: West-Malling railway station

Also nearby
St. Mary's Church M19 6NE
Manor Park Country Park ME19 6PE

West Malling is a delightful small town with picturesque historic buildings, including some very nice pubs. St. Leonard's Street leads out of town to the south west, and passes right by the tower.

In some earlier books it states that the tower had become derelict and was impossible to enter. More recently however, local volunteers mounted a rescue programme and a small information board standing just outside the tower states that it was possible to get inside the tower at any reasonable time by making an appointment with the parish council. Unfortunately, if you arrive unexpectedly for a quick visit it is probably too late to contact them. Information from various websites suggests that it is now open to anyone during the working day. You will probably have to take your chance, but whether you get in or not, it is still worth a look.

History
The tower takes its name from a chapel, dedicated to Saint Leonard, which once stood nearby, but apart from that there is not much known about it. Some believe that it is the last surviving part of a castle which was built by Gundulf, Bishop of Rochester between 1077 and 1108. Others believe the castle was built by William the Conqueror's half-brother, Bishop Odo of Bayeux. My own opinion is somewhat less grand, that it may have belonged to St. Mary's Abbey, which was less than half a mile away where the church of St. Mary the Virgin now stands.

West-Malling: Saint Leonards Tower, South Western Elevation.

Description and Defences

Saint Leonards Tower is a three storied tower or small keep, 10 meters wide on each side and approximately 20 meters high. The walls are around 2 meters thick which would be sufficient to protect against robbers or rioting peasants, but not against an army. A spiral staircase in the north-west turret connects the basement to the two upper floors. The windows are rounded at the top, the normal design for the Norman period.

The original entrance was above ground level and had to be reached by an external wooden staircase. It also has arrow slits. These features suggest it had a defensive purpose, and yet the windows are larger than we would expect in a proper castle. As there are neither fireplaces nor latrines it seems unlikely that the castle was built to be lived in. It may be, therefore, that the tower was part of a manor house or small castle and was intended as a place of refuge in an emergency. Such buildings are commonly found in the north of England where they are called peel towers or pele towers. It seems likely that in the years just after the Norman Conquest the authorities might have felt the need for need similar places of safety in the south. In fact a similar structure, Gundulf's Tower, was built near Rochester Cathedral for that very reason.

From the north-east corner of the tower a section of medieval wall runs off to the east and this could have been the boundary of a yard or enclosure around the tower, but it is not sufficiently high or wide to be classed as a castle wall.

West-Malling: Saint Leonards Tower, South Eastern Elevation.

Westenhanger Castle

A major medium structure in Hythe, owned by the local council.
Postcode for Satnav: CT21 4HX
Nearest major road   M20
Website: https://www.westenhangercastle.co.uk/
Parking Arrangements: Free on-site for wedding guests
Public transport: Westenhanger railway station.

Also nearby
Lympne Castle
Port Lympne Safari Park
Crypt of St. Leonard's Church, Hythe.

Some old books and documents refer to Westenhanger and others refer to Oestenhanger, which creates a certain amount of confusion. These are not alternative spellings of the same name. Rather there was an area known as "Le Hangre" which had once belonged personally to King Canute, and it was later divided into two manors, Eastern Hangre and Western Hangre. Later they were re-combined into a single property, for which both names have been used, rather whimsically at times.

Description and Defences
The castle once had a moat, up to 15 meters wide, which was fed by the river Stour but is now dry.

The curtain wall was rectangular in shape, though not quite square, because it was fitted into the existing island made by the moat, with square towers in the middle of each wall and round towers on each corner, except for the south-east one which was square. The gate-house had both a drawbridge and a portcullis.

History
In 1344, King Edward III granted John de Kiriel a licence to crenellate his manor house at Westenhanger, near Folkestone. New walls were built on an existing site, fitting inside a moat fed by the River Stour.

There is a local tradition that Rosamund Clifford, is said to have lived at the manor house for a while. Known as "Fair Rosamund" and also as "The Rose of the World," she was regarded as one of the most beautiful women of the 12th Century. She became the Mistress of King Henry II, the father of Richard the Lionheart. When her affair with the king ended she retired to Godstow Abbey, where she died in 1176, at the age of just 30 years.

The north-west tower of Westenhanger castle is known as Rosamund's Tower, on the assumption that she lived there, though in fact this is most unlikely as she died one and a half centuries before the towers were built. It may be that she had stayed at the manor before it was fortified. Whatever the facts, this local legend adds just a little romance to the setting.

Westenhanger Castle

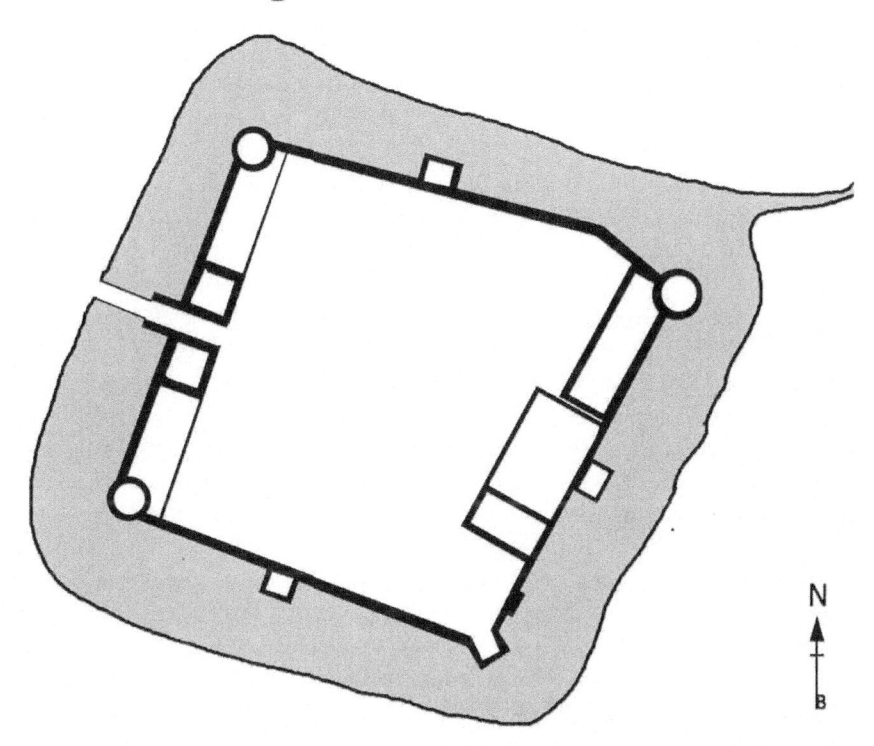

Another story regarding the castle was less romantic but, perhaps, even more entertaining. Eventually Sir John Kiriel died, leaving a widow, with the rather unusual name of Lady Lettice Kiriel, and his son Nicholas Kiriel who was himself married with a baby son. Nicholas, however, died young and so Lady Lettice was left to manage the estate on behalf of her infant grandson.

In 1382 a landless knight by the name of Sir John Cornwall besieged the castle, with a small band of nine retainers, intending to kidnap the baby and his grandmother, in order to gain control of the estate. During the night they scaled the walls using just ladders, which suggests that the Kiriels did not actually have much in the way of fighting forces to defend the castle. They then broke into the various buildings and rooms, but somehow Lady Lettice managed to hide. Some accounts suggest she had prior knowledge of the attack. Others even say that she plunged neck-deep into the lake, which must have been both dangerous and unpleasant for a middle aged grandmother. Whatever the details, the attackers were unable to find her. Eventually they left having robbed the place, and stolen the horses. Sir John and his companions were later charged for their behaviour.

The castle remained with the de Kiriel family until 1461, when Sir Thomas Kiriel was executed after the battle of St. Albans. It later passed to one of their descendants, Sir Edward Poyning. Henry VIII then took a fancy to it and obtained it from Poyning as part of a land deal. Henry improved and extended the property to the point where some studies estimate it had more than a hundred rooms. Sadly all of this grandeur was stripped away in the years which followed.

In the Elizabethan period the crown held the castle until it was granted to Thomas Smythe in 1585 as a reward for his good service. Smythe was one of the early entrepreneurs of the capitalist system, so adept in his wheeling and dealing that he acquired the nick-name "Customer Smythe."

His son, also Thomas Smythe, commissioned the building of a twenty ton ship named "The Discovery" which sailed to Virginia with the "Godspeed" and the "Susan Constant" to found the first British colony in the Americas at Jamestown. A replica of the Discovery is now on show in the castle.

In 1691 the castle was damaged by an earthquake, a rare event in England. This was the start of a downward spiral and as is the case with so many castles, it eventually fell into disrepair. Parts of it were demolished for building materials and of the original nine towers only two survived. The property itself was used for agricultural purposes. In fact, it seems likely that one of the towers only survived intact because it was being used as a dovecot. During that period pigeons were kept in large numbers in order to be used for cooking. It is, perhaps, rather ironic that what is now an important listed building only survived because some character in days gone by wanted to enjoy a nice pigeon pie now and then.

By 1957 the whole site was considered to be a building at risk and then ion 1987 it suffered damage in the "Great Storm.," particularly affecting the roof of the barn.

By 1980 the entire structure was overgrown by ivy and there was a real danger that it could have been lost completely. Fortunately it was purchased by new owners in 1996 who began the task of restoration, particularly as regards to its historical barn. Originally built in Elizabethan times, it was built from Kentish Ragstone but had a "Hammerbeam Roof." This is a complex structure made from oak beams which was completely restored between 2007 and 2010, by the new owners, the Forge family, with financial support from English Heritage.

Bruce W. Johnson

In 2019 the castle was purchased by Folkestone and Hythe Council, and is in now use as a conference centre and high quality wedding venue at the heart of a 100 acre leisure park and nature reserve. This may seem to be a very satisfactory outcome for a historical building which was previously seen as being at risk of destruction, however there were some who opposed the intervention of the council;

https://www.kentonline.co.uk/folkestone/news/backlash-after-council-buys-castle-211821/

In 2022 plans were unveiled to create a "Garden City" in the Otterpoopl Park area. Westenhanger Castle is intended to be within the boundaries of the new scheme but, of course, it will be fully preserved.

Whitstable Castle

A major structure in Whitstable. Owned by the local council.
Postcode for Satnav: CT5 2BW
Nearest major road   IS
Website: https://www.whitstablecastle.co.uk/

History
Whitstable was not a medieval castle. Around 1780 a local businessman, named Charles Pearson, built a mock-gothic octagonal tower with good views out over the sea. Over the years more buildings were added, creating an extensive and picturesque mock-gothic residence.

Whitstable Castle from the air.

In 1935 the local council purchased the castle to use as offices.
Following the local government re-organisation in 1972, the Castle stood empty. Then in 1975 The Whitstable Society the "Castle Centre Association" was created with the aim of using The Castle for the benefit of the people of Whitstable, although the building was still owned by the council.
In 2004 the committee began a complete interior upgrade and secured KCC 'Approved Venue' status for Weddings and Civil Ceremonies. This brought in much needed income to regenerate the Castle and enable it to return to its original role as a venue for family celebrations, major local events and community activities. In 2008 a new Trust was formed to take over the

running of the Castle and Gardens with support from a heritage Lottery Grant.

Although the castle is a relatively modern structure it does look impressive and has won a place in the heart of the local people. With its romantic towers and its sunny gardens it fits perfectly into the ambience of a traditional seaside town.

At the time of writing [2022] the castle clearly serves the community in many ways, with all sorts of events taking place, from antique fairs and murder mystery evenings to Christmas parties and Santa's Grotto. It is also a popular wedding venue. [See website for details]

Whitstable Castle and back steps from the rear gardens.

Minor Castle Sites

I have chosen to omit a small number of castle sites from this book. In some cases all that remains are slight earthworks, mounds and ditches in a field. There are also some sites which I have not listed in this book because there are no longer any remains at all. Some will have been built over, while others were completely dismantled and their stones re-used.

I have therefore decided not to include a site if there is so little left that a visit might prove to be disappointing.

Among those which I passed over are;

Knox Bridge Castle
Newnham Castle
Tonge Castle

For information on these more obscure sites I recommend the Gatehouse listing which covers all of the counties in England.

http://www.gatehouse-gazetteer.info/home.html

Bruce W. Johnson

Planning your visits

Kent is very fortunate to have so many surviving castles in such good condition. However, some castles were only ever built from earth and timber others have been demolished and their stones used for building projects. Some survive only as ruins, sometimes nothing more than a grassy mound or a muddy ditch in a field. They may not be what you are looking for when planning a day out. In order to avoid disappointment you should always check the details as given in this book before planning a visit.

It also makes sense to visit one area at a time, so that you spend as little time as possible travelling and as much time as possible enjoying your sightseeing.

On the pages which follow you will find suggestions for several different tours of Kent Castles;

1. The London Area
2. North Kent
3. Leeds Castle and Central Kent
4. East Kent
5. West Kent
6. The Very Best
7. Ornamental Gardens
8. The Grand Tour

Where appropriate I have included details of other attractions, such as museums, cathedrals and palaces, and of castles which may be just outside of the county but so close that they are worth including.

I have also mentioned a few places where it is possible to stay as a resident in a castle or other historical building, for those occasions when you fancy a really great romantic experience, however I would always recommend you to do your own research as there are plenty of other hotels available, and living in a castle is never going to be the cheapest option!

Tour 1: The London Area

The Tower of London
Hampton Court Palace and gardens.
Kensington Palace and gardens.
Buckingham Palace, only open certain days - see website.
Windsor Castle and Windsor Great Park.
Eltham Palace and gardens.
Kew Palace and gardens.
Vanbrugh House, not open to public but near Greenwich Park.
Severndroog Tower only open selected days but set in natural woodland.
Bromley Palace, not open to the public, but set in pleasant park.

Only half of these buildings are actually in Kent, but they are all in the London area which overlaps Kent. Of greater importance, they can all be reached by public transport, so that if you are visiting London but do not have a car you can still include them in your sightseeing. All of them have ornamental gardens or park lands nearby, providing opportunities for a pleasant day out.

These are some of the greatest historical buildings in Britain but in many cases they are still in use for ceremonial events, and even by members of the royal family, so it is always important to check their websites for exact details of opening times.

Vanbrugh is a private house and Bromley Palace is now used as office space by the local authorities, so neither of these is ever open to tourists, however they are both near to nice parks and are worth taking a look at, if you happen to be passing.

Other London buildings with historical value include Westminster Abbey, St. Pauls Cathedral and the monument to the Great Fire of London.

Three famous museums, the Science Museum, the Natural History Museum, and the Victoria and Albert Museum, are all very close to one another so it is possible to visit more than one on the same day. Other museums include the Imperial War Museum, the National Army Museum, (Chelsea) and the London Dungeon.

Bruce W. Johnson

Tour 2: Leeds Castle and Central Kent

Drive to Rochester on your first morning, arrive early and find good parking - there are several car parks near the castle and the High Street, and a lot to see, as detailed in this book.

In the afternoon drive on to Leeds Castle.

On the next day enjoy Leeds Castle to the full. If you are there for bed and breakfast you can get into the castle as soon as it opens, and be ahead of the crowds who will start arriving from the car park about twenty minutes later.

Leeds Castle by Morris

Leeds has its own top-quality restaurant on site. There is also a pub just round the corner called the Park Gate Inn which also serves meals There is so much to see at Leeds that you will probably want to revisit some of the attractions again the following day, alternatively you could go to visit the ornamental gardens at Sissinghurst.

On the way back from Leeds towards London you have the option to take a quick look at several smaller sites; St. Leonards Tower in West Malling, Leybourne Castle, Otford, Lullingstone or Eynsford.

Tour 3: North Kent

Upnor Castle
Rochester Castle [Full day recommended]
Gundulph's Tower
Rochester Cathedral,
Chatham Historic Naval Dockyard
Fort Amherst, Gillingham
Leeds Castle [Full day recommended]

Most of the sites listed are close to the Medway Towns area, but at the time of writing there were no castles in the locality which provided accommodation. However, I did recently visit the "Ship and Trades Hotel" which stands in the heart of the area which was once the Royal Dockyard at Chatham. It is in an interesting location; close to the historic dockyard museum, but also in the heart of a large modern shopping mall.

Make Upnor Castle the main visit of your first day, [but check in advance that it will be open] then on to your hotel.

On the following days there is plenty to do in the Rochester area. The Castle itself stands close to the Cathedral and Rochester High Street is delightful, with many historic buildings linked to the life and works of Charles Dickens.

The historic Royal Dockyard and/or Fort Amherst will occupy you for another day.

On your final day drive to Leeds Castle and spend the day there, or even book to stay there if you have an extra day.

On the way back from Leeds towards London you have the option to take a quick look at several smaller sites such as St. Leonards Tower, [West Malling] Leybourne, Otford, Lullingstone or Eynsford.

Touring North Kent

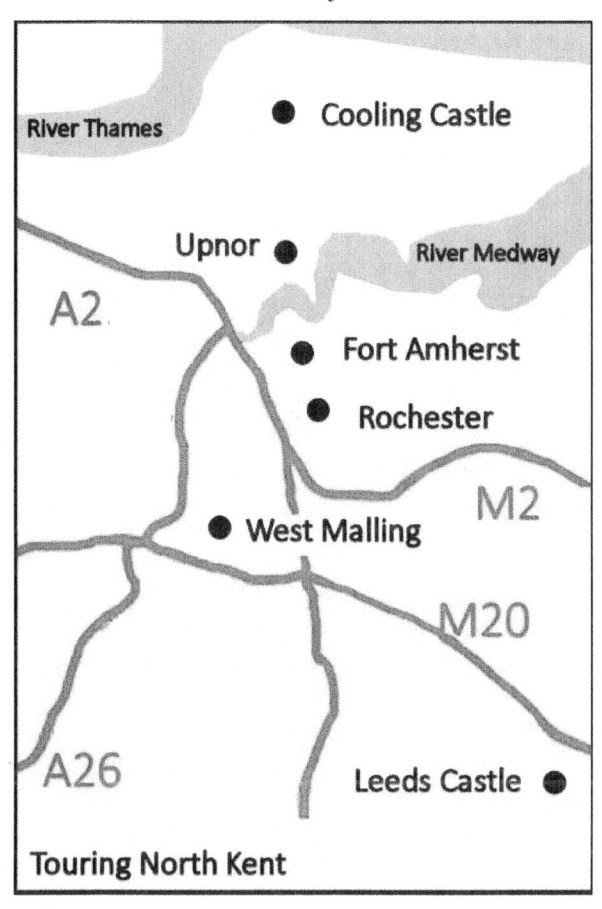

Tour 4: East Kent

Canterbury [Full day recommended]
Sandwich
Richborough
Walmer and Deal
Dover Castle [Full day recommended]

Canterbury Castle is impressive for its size, but in a poor state of repair and you will probably spend only a few minutes there. However there are so many other things to see in Canterbury that you can easily spend a whole day in the city. Details of the buildings are given in this book. There are also boat trips and numerous quaint shops as well as nice places to eat.

Sandwich is a gorgeous medieval town and a useful base for visiting the Roman ruins at Richborough and the Tudor fortresses at Walmer and Deal. There is also "Old Walmer Court" tucked away in the streets just back from the sea front. Dover Castle could arguably claim the title of the most impressive fortress in Britain, being both massive and well preserved. It was once called "The Key to England" and has continued to be used as a front-line defence from Roman times until the present day. Allow a whole day for Dover.

On your way home you have the option of looking at several castles which are not open to the public but can be seen from the outside. Sandgate, Saltwood Castle, Westenhanger Castle and the Dymchurch Redoubt are all situated to the west of Dover. Lympne Castle is best viewed from the ruins of Stutfall, which lies in the fields beneath it.

The eastern region of Kent has recently become a very popular area with young people who wish to buy a house which is outside of London and close to the seaside. This has added to the social and cultural life of the area. Kent also enjoys a longstanding reputation as a traditional holiday destination. This means there is no shortage of places to stay.

Personally, I favour the delightful small town of Sandwich where the Bell Hotel is well positioned on the quayside and the New Inn overlooks the historic market. Just outside of the town another hotel, The Blazing Donkey comes highly recommended.

Bruce W. Johnson

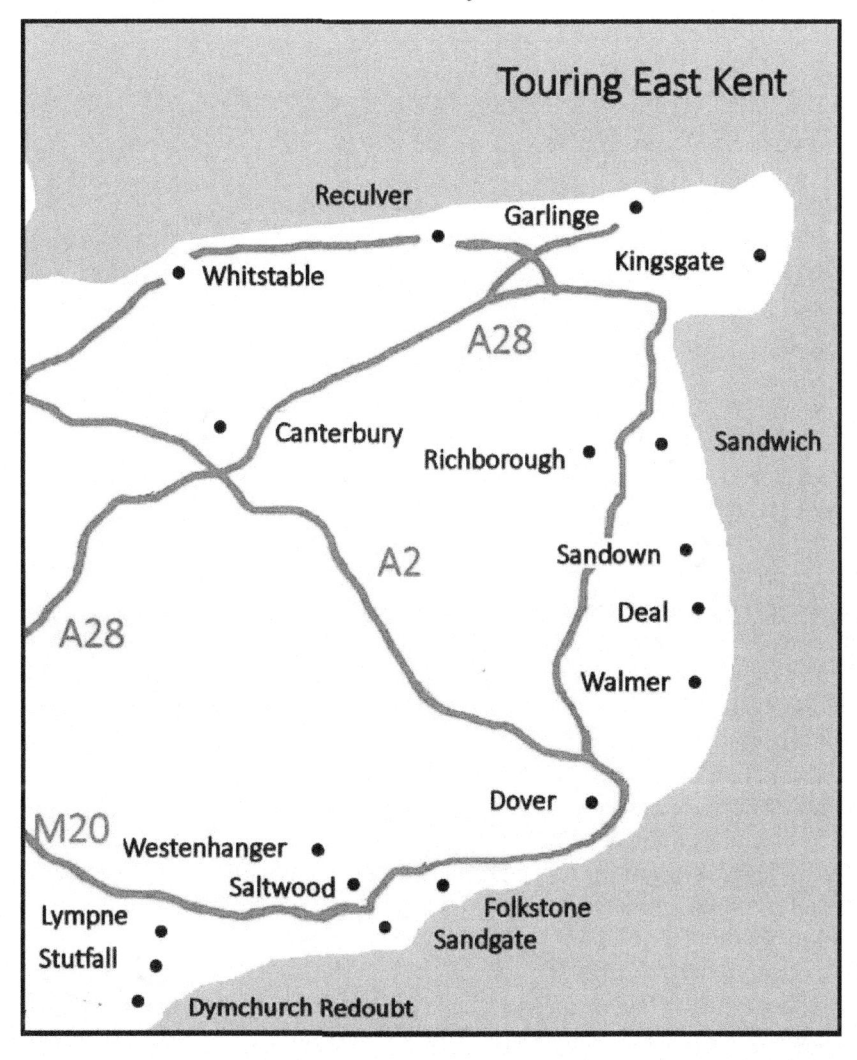

Touring East Kent

Tour 5: West Kent

Eynsford
Lullingstone
Hever Castle [Full day recommended]
Penshurst Place
Ightham Mote
Knole
Scotney
Tonbridge
Hadlow
Old Soar

Travelling down into Kent via the M25 and A 21 it is possible to call in on Eynsford castle and then visit Lullingstone where you have the opportunity to visit three attractions in the same place. Lullingstone Castle is worthy of attention in itself, but the site also hosts a project known as the "World Garden." Meanwhile, on the same stretch of road, it is possible to visit Lullingstone Roman Villa.

West Kent is particularly favoured with well-preserved castles and stately homes. There are three reasons for this. Initially, castles in the county were fortified against the risk of French invasion. Later, the south east of England sided with parliament in the English Civil War, so fewer of the local castles were destroyed. Finally, in more recent times, wealthy individuals have chosen to preserve and restore these great buildings which provide grand houses in an area not far from London. Hever Castle is an example of all three factors and of all the places I have ever stayed in the world it is my firm favourite. When you have finished your tour of the castle I strongly advise you to walk all the way down through the Italian Gardens to the lake. It is a beautiful location, especially in good weather.

Knole and Penshurst place are ideal for those who prefer a stately home to a castle. On the way back you could stop for a coffee in Chiddingstone which is a beautiful small village, entirely owned by the National Trust.

Ightham Mote is a fortified manor house rather than a castle but it is outstanding for many reasons, and should definitely be on your agenda.

Scotney Castle has beautiful gardens and a romantic ruined tower, perfect for a very special photo-shot,

Travelling back after your holiday, there is the option to follow the A 26 and to stop off briefly at Tonbridge Castle, Hadlow, Old Soar Manor House and Leybourne Castle. Hadlow is a folly, and only open on a very restricted number of days, but worth seeing all the same.

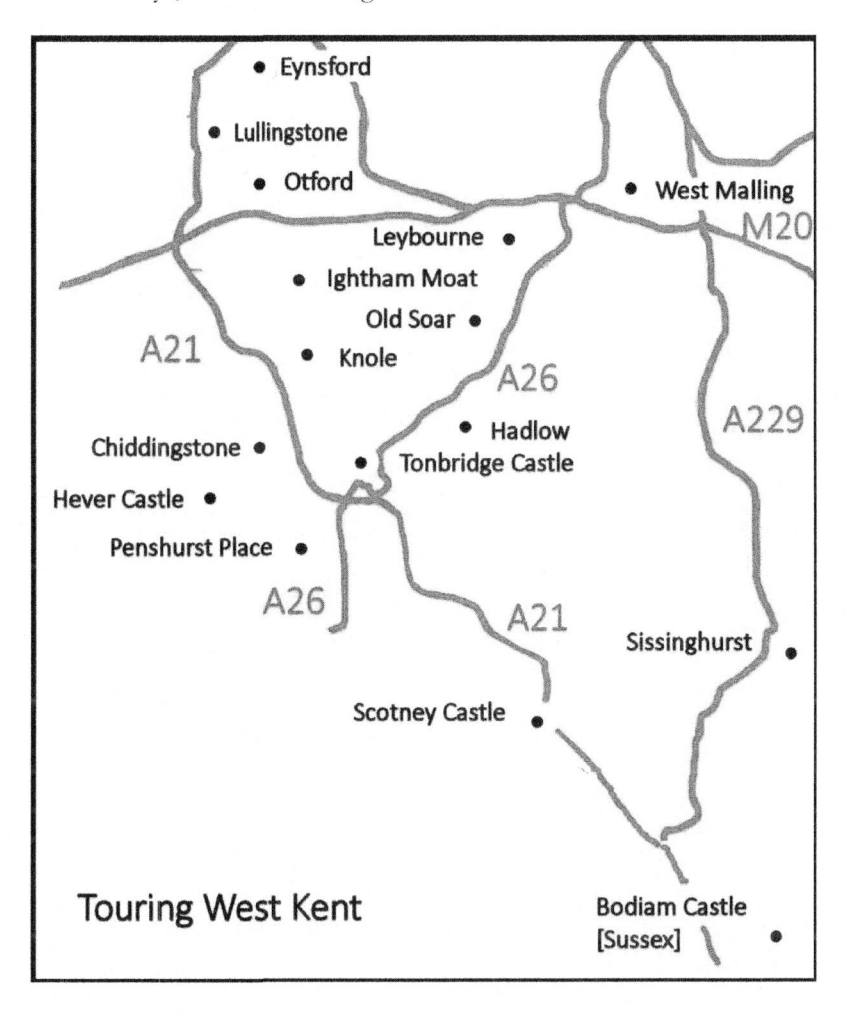

Touring West Kent

Tour 6: The very best

Rochester Castle and High Street
Leeds Castle
Canterbury City
Dover Castle
Ightham Mote
Knole
Hever Castle
Penshurst Place

If you could only visit Kent for one week in your whole lifetime, these are the sites you should try not to miss. Each one of them provides so much to see that they all deserve a full day to visit. It is possible that you could view Rochester on your way down and then stay at a central location, travelling to each one on a different day. I have stayed at Eastwell Manor, near Ashford, which provides an excellent base and also has a luxury spa. Alternatively, if you are prepared to make an effort in your bookings, it should be possible to stay overnight in several historical venues, including Leeds Castle and Hever Castle.

Bruce W. Johnson

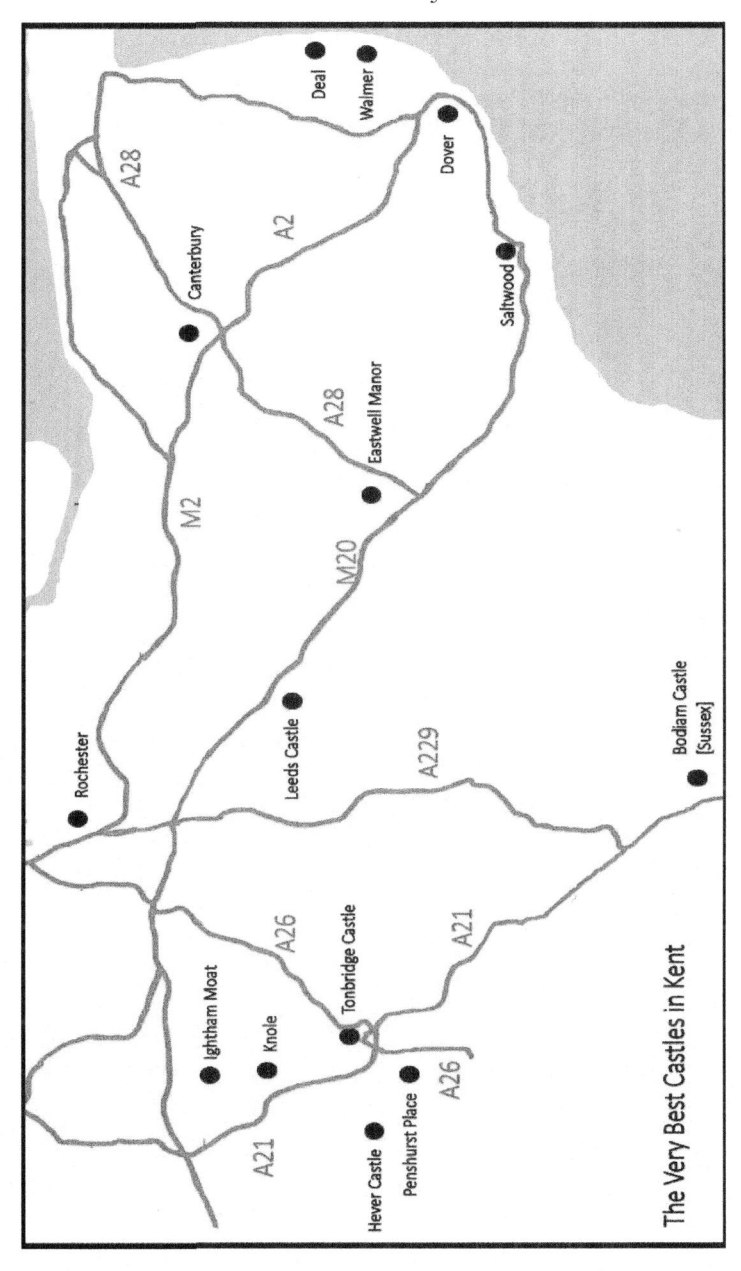

The Very Best Castles in Kent

Tour 7: Ornamental Gardens

Lullingstone Castle and World Garden
Hever Castle
Chiddingstone Village and Castle Gardens
Penshurst Place
Sissinghurst Castle and Gardens.
Scotney Castle.

Kent is sometimes described as the Garden of England, and for those who enjoy an easy day visiting beautiful landscaped gardens it has plenty to offer.

If gardens are your passion then Hever Castle would be a perfect place to stay. All of the others, listed above, are in the same general area.

Bruce W. Johnson

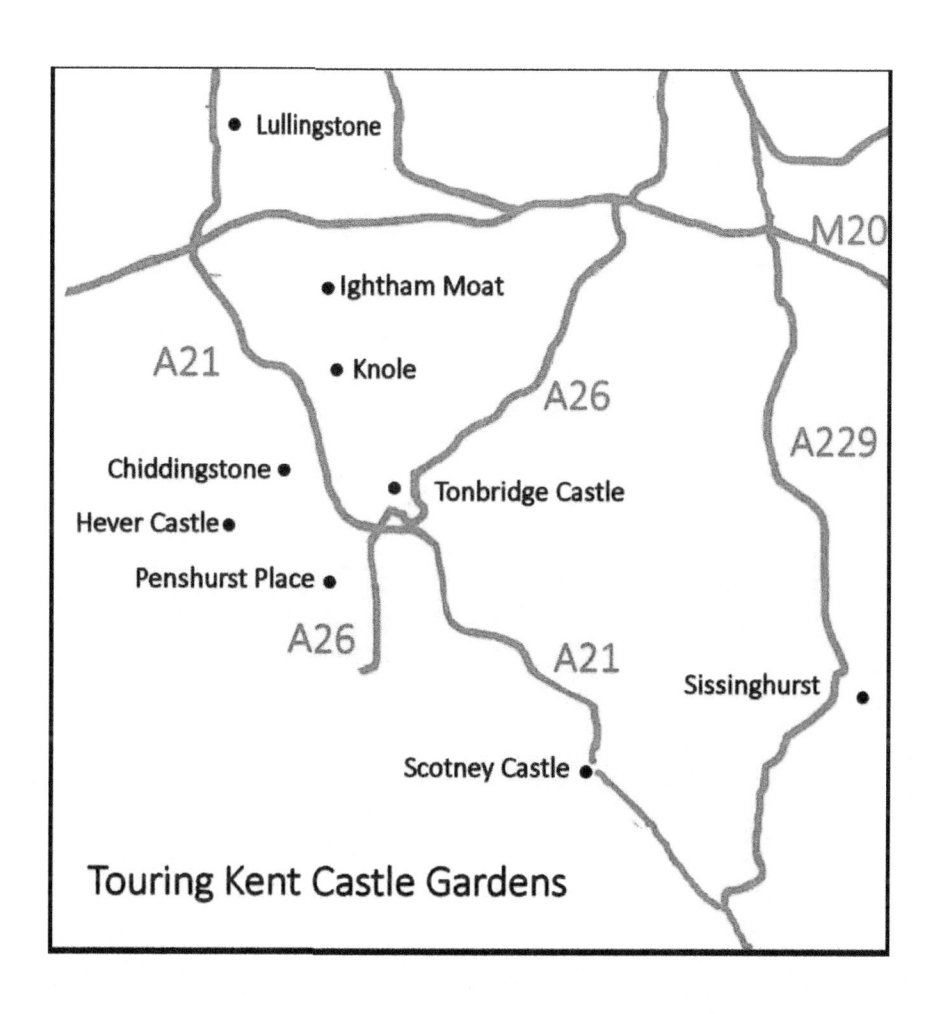

Touring Kent Castle Gardens

Tour 8: The Grand Tour

Upnor Castle,
Chatham Naval Dockyard
Rochester Castle,
Fort Amherst Redoubt
Canterbury Castle, City Walls and West Gate
Walmer and Deal,
Richborough
Dover Castle
Westenhanger Castle,
Saltwood Castle,
Sandgate Castle
Lympne Castle
Stutfall Castle.
Leeds Castle
Hever Castle.
Ightham Mote
Penshurst Place
Lullingstone Castle, World Garden and Roman Villa.
Otford Palace
Eynsford Castle

For someone who is free to spend more than a week, this circular tour takes in all of the most significant castles in Kent. I have kept it to nine days, but you could extend it further simply by booking an extra night here and there. I would, however, urge you to book a very long way in advance. Some of the accommodation is very popular.

Travelling round Kent in a clockwise direction;

Book 2 nights' accommodation in Medway Towns, 2 nights in Sandwich or one of the coastal towns, 1 or 2 nights at Leeds Castle or Eastwell Manor and the remainder at Hever Castle or the surrounding area.

Day 1. Travel down into Kent on the A2 visiting Upnor Castle and Chatham Naval Dockyard then spending the night in Medway
Day 2. Visit Rochester Castle and the Fort Amherst Redoubt spending the night in Medway.

Day 3. Leave Medway and travel by the A2 to Canterbury to see the castle, city walls, cathedral, west gate and other attractions. Spend the night in Canterbury or Sandwich or any resort on the coast.

Day 4. Day trip to Walmer and Deal, possibly Richborough as well. Spend the night in Canterbury or Sandwich or any resort on the coast.

Day 5. Leave accommodation and visit Dover Castle for the whole day, then set off towards Leeds Castle, with the option of taking a peek at Westenhanger Castle, Saltwood Castle, and Sandgate Castle which are all very close to one another. Lympne Castle is also in the area but is not open to the public and best viewed from the ruins of Stutfall Castle.
Spend the night at Leeds Castle, or Eastwell Manor.

Day 6. View Leeds Castle, sometimes called the most beautiful castle in England. Spend the night at Leeds or move on towards Hever.

Day 7 Spend the day at Hever Castle. The building and its gardens are both magnificent. Spend the night at Hever.

Day 8 Visit Ightham Mote and on the way back stop off at Chiddingstone Village. Spend the night at Hever.

Day 9 Visit Penshurst Place, then travel home with the options of stopping off at Lullingstone, Otford or Eynsford.

Bruce W. Johnson

Places to stay

Kent has long been a popular holiday destination and there is no shortage of places to stay. The following suggestions are primarily for those readers who wish to enter further into the spirit of touring castles, by staying at places which have a degree of historical grandeur.

I have no financial connection to any of these establishments, and include their details only for your convenience.

North Kent
Ship and Trades Hotel, St Mary's Island, Chatham ME4 3ER
Cooling Castle Barn has accommodation for guests attending weddings.

Central Kent
Leeds Castle, near Maidstone.
Eastwell Manor, near Ashford.
A luxurious hotel set in a medieval manor-house. It also includes a beautiful modern spa.

West Kent
Hever Castle

East Kent
The New Inn, Sandwich
The Bell Hotel, Sandwich
The Blazing Donkey, Sandwich
Howfield Manor, Canterbury

South Kent
Lympne Castle [Self catering holiday cottages.]

A wedding in the Great Hall of Allington Castle.

Bruce W. Johnson

Weddings and Venues

Several of the castles and other venues mentioned in this book are available as wedding venues, film sets, and conference centres.

The following list was correct at the time of writing but obviously you should check the official websites as these things tend to change with the passage of time.

Allington Castle
Bromley Palace Civic Centre
Bradbourne House
Chatham Historic Dockyard
Chiddingstone Castle
Chilham Castle
Cooling Castle Barn
Eastwell Manor
Hever Castle
Leeds Castle
Lympne Castle
Penshurst Place
Scotney Castle
Severndroog Tower
Sissinghurst Castle and Gardens
Westenhanger Castle
Whitstable Castle

Cycle Repairs

Options for cycle repairs are prone to change as new shops open and others close.

There are, however, a number of websites which offer up to date listings, some of which I have included below. I have no financial connection to any of these organisations.

https://www.sustrans.org.uk/campaigns/bike-shops-near-me/

https://bikebook.co.uk/

https://www.halfords.com/bikes/services/halfords-bike-repairs.html

Bruce W. Johnson

List of Illustrations

Allington Castle Kent
Allington Castle in 1909 by Lord Conway
Allington Castle: Plan *
Allington Castle: The Great Hall courtesy of Allington Castle
Bromley Palace 1756
Canterbury Keep Plan *
Canterbury Castle and City Walls Plan *
Canterbury West Gate: 2009 *
Castle Toll, location map.
Chiddingstone Village *
Chilham Castle: Print by Watts 1785
Chilham Castle Lieven Smits
Chilham Castle Plan *
Cooling Castle Plan *
Cooling Castle from a print by Buck c1735
Cooling Castle tower and moat *
Cooling Castle gun port *
Cooling Castle gatehouse *
Cooling Castle gatehouse machicolations *
Cooling Castle gatehouse towers *
Cooling Castle gatehouse towers Hooper 1784
Deal Castle from a print by Daniel 1823
Deal Castle Plan *
Dover Castle Keep Plan *
Eastwell Manor *
Eynsford Castle Plan *
Garlinge Castle: Victorian Postcard
Hadlow Castle photograph 1890
Hever Castle, watercolour by Henry Bright 1870
Hever Castle Plan *
Hever Castle courtyard by Nash c1840
Hever Castle, the gallery, by Nash c1840
Hever Castle The Long Gallery c. Hever Castle

Ightham Village *
Ightham Moat Plan *
Kingsgate Castle RodW
Knole by Morris c1750
Knole by Nash 1840
Knole, the bedchamber, by Nash 1840
Leeds Castle viewed across the moat
Leeds Castle Plan *
Leeds Castle situated in moat, aerial image
Lullingstone Castle
Lullingstone Castle, world garden.
Lympne Castle Plan *
Lympne Castle, Photograph 1903
Lympne Castle from Stutfall 2022
Mereworth Castle, detail, by Neale 1825
Otford Palace Plan *
Penshurst Place, sketch by Neale c1825
Penshurst Place, Great Hall, by Nash c1840
Queenborough Castle, by Hooper 1748
Queenborough Castle Plan *
Reculver Roman Fort Plan *
Reculver Church c1660 photo sketch *
Plan of Richborough Roman Fort *
Rochester Castle 2010*
Rochester Castle Keep 2010 *
Saltwood Castle by Deeble 1818
Saltwood Castle Plan *
Saltwood Castle 1830
Sandgate Castle, Newton 1787
Sandgate Castle Plan *
Scotney Castle Plan *
Severndroog Tower by Brayley c1815
Shurland Hall, photo sketch 2022 *
Shurland Hall Plan *
Sissinghurst c1700
Sissinghurst photo sketch 2022
Stone Castle 2022 *
Sutton Valence Castle Plan *
Sutton Valence Castle *
Tonbridge Castle, by Baines c1829
Tonbridge Castle Plan *
Upnor Castle photo sketch 2022 *
Walmer Castle Plan *

Bruce W. Johnson

West-Malling: Saint Leonards Tower SW elevation *
West-Malling: Saint Leonards Tower SE elevation *
Westenhanger Castle Plan *
Whitstable Castle Aerial View by Harry Walker
Whitstable Castle
Canterbury: The Weavers Cottages 2009 *
Rochester: Redbrick buildings 2010 *
Leeds Castle by Morris c1750

* Copyright of the author.

Acknowledgements

The author wishes to thank all those staff, at various castles, who shared their knowledge of the sites.

In particular, thanks are offered for the use of photographs, as follows:

Allington Castle photographed in 1909 by Lord Conway, courtesy of Kent Archaeological Society.
External image of Allington Castle Kent, public domain, licensed under Wikimedia Creative Commons Licence, CC BY-SA 4.0, https://commons.wikimedia.org/w/index.php?curid=41762690
Allington Castle: Images of the Great Hall, by courtesy of Allington Castle.
Chilham Castle aerial photo by Lieven Smits reproduced under the conditions of the GNU Free Documentation Licence [Lieven@ster.be]
Hever Castle, The Long gallery by courtesy of Hever Castle
Kingsgate Castle by Rodw - Public Domain image.
Leeds Castle across the moat, courtesy of Leeds Castle
Leeds Castle aerial image, courtesy of Leeds Castle
Lullingsone Castle Gatehouse by courtesy of Lullingstone Castle, photo credit Alan Graham.
Lullingstone World Garden by courtesy of Lullingstone Castle, photo credit Stephen Sangster
Whitstable Castle, aerial view by courtesy of Whitstable Castle, photo credit Harry Walker
Whitstable Castle, view of back steps, by courtesy of Whitstable Castle

Printed in Great Britain
by Amazon